DECORATE
your GARDEN

DECORATE
your GARDEN

Affordable Ideas and Ornaments for Small Gardens

MARY KEEN

PHOTOGRAPHS BY MARIJKE HEUFF

conran
OCTOPUS

First published in Great Britain in 1993 by
Conran Octopus Limited
37 Shelton Street
London, WC2H 9HN
a part of Octopus Publishing Group
www.conran-octopus.co.uk

Reprinted 1994, 1998
This paperback edition published in 1999

British Library Cataloguing-in-Publication Data
A catalogue record for this book is available from the British Library.

ISBN 1-84091-063-1

Plant identification Tony Lord

Art Director Mary Evans
Picture Research Jessica Walton
Senior Editor Sarah Pearce
Art Editor and DTP David Rowley Design
Text Editor Sarah Riddell
Editorial Assistant Charlottte Coleman-Smith
Production Sonya Sibbons

Printed in China

Contents

Between the realms of urns and gnomes lies uncharted territory.
Garden decorations can be as idiosyncratic or as individual as you
choose to make them.

Introduction

Garden ornament is a heavyweight, going on for monumental, subject. The words suggest the trappings of grandeur destined for Renaissance princes or Edwardian magnates, evoking a world far beyond the aspirations of today's gardeners. The frivolous end of the ornament spectrum is occupied by gnomes, which have a reputation for being not quite the thing. Between urns and gnomes lies uncharted territory; it is this area that the book explores. Urns will appear and so will gnomes, but what we hope is that these pages will open eyes and kick-start imaginations.

LEFT Miniature narcissi in a pot have been made to look even more important by putting them on a pedestal. With the table and the flowers sharing the same shade of colour, the whole arrangement is unified and turned into a set piece.
ABOVE The plants in shallow pans raised on chimney pots are easy to see as they make their inconsequential procession down lines of feathered cobbles.

Gardens are essentially private areas where the spirit of the place and the imagination of the owner are joined in creating the perfect backdrop for place and person. For this aim, in a way, small gardens have the edge on public ones, which are geared to pleasing lots of people. Gardens that are open to visitors tend to be arranged to suit spectators rather than dreamers, but private gardens can have deep meanings designed to be absorbed on lonely strolls. Unity of vision, from one pair of eyes, can control all that is seen in a private plot so that it becomes a place that reflects reflections, a map of personal preferences. Ornaments have traditionally been the props to rely on as prompts to the imagination; they still have the power to turn thoughts and mould moods. But what worked for our ancestors – the urn that suggested mortality, the statue that reminded the onlooker of classical heroism – no longer works for us today. Their message is now overlaid with associations of a grandeur that is gone, so that when we look at a statue of Apollo or Diana, we see not a god or a goddess but stone figures from the past. If they are to work for us, fresh images that speak to the present must be found. For some, the abandoned boat on page 82 will say as much about the passage of

time as a funerary urn would have said to an eighteenth-century gardener. For others, the petals falling from the magnolia on pages 14-15 will summon an equally powerful *memento mori*.

The primary value of ornament in the garden is that it can be used to suggest feelings. Plants can do this too, but objects are better. The cleaned spades in the potting shed that imply honest toil, the souvenir shells and stones brought home from seaside places, the plant from a friend's garden, are all more than they seem to be. The definition of 'souvenir' has been eroded so that it has come to mean little more than a trophy of a place, but a souvenir is literally something that brings back a memory.

If this engineering of associations leaves you cold, there are other ways of decorating the garden. Utilitarian objects like seats and pots and watering cans can be beautiful as well as useful. Adapt the William Morris precept that only those things that are beautiful or useful deserve a place in the home, and combine both qualities in everything that you choose to work with out of doors.

Of course there is a place for beauty that has neither use nor association, and the garden is possibly one of the few settings where beauty

ABOVE Trim box hedges are a garden cliché but plenty of less well known plants can be grown as formal hedges. Where a hedge is needed as a feature, coloured leaves make a change from evergreen ones, which tend to merge into the background. This square of purple berberis stands out sharply against a haze of greens and yellows. Purple leaves look good with plum-coloured brick like those on the ground, and this particular shrub is so prickly that it acts as a deterrent to animals and children. For this reason, berberis is often chosen in town plantings where vandalism is a threat. (Roses and holly also make formidable hedges.)

Low hedges can often sharpen up and define the planting by providing a frame to surround the flowers. This simple device will strengthen weak plantings and also help to conceal untidy herbs or the bare legs of roses.

can be strictly for the eye of the beholder. It can be the place to enjoy home-made artworks, the objects that other people fail to recognize as beautiful but that you secretly always liked. Gnomes come into this category, so do curious plants, lumps of topiary, scarecrows and things made by children.

Gardens are a combination of the settled and the ephemeral. If they feel like places where the world stops and nothing ever happens, they also have their share of surprises, as flowers come and go. If the element of change appeals more to you than the static timelessness of a garden, this can be heightened by temporary displays of objects. Put them somewhere where only you can see them (not in the view enjoyed by others) and they will be a private source of pleasure. Simple effects, like a row of found pebbles on a low wall, a group of pots near a door, a dramatic plant in an unlikely place, an improvised wall fountain, can all change the emphasis in the way you look at a garden. And when they no longer seem as fresh as they once did, the focus can be shifted to another area. Indoors, if you wanted to add to the pleasure of being at home, you might put flowers on a table, hang a picture in a different place, or change the colour of a cushion. Outside, similar tricks can be

ABOVE LEFT Free-standing but firmly anchored plant supports allow climbers to be grown in the open, away from walls and fences. Clematis is one of the best plants for clothing small supports in a short time. Here it is seen on an aluminium frame that will also make a contribution to the garden in winter.

ABOVE RIGHT Here is a modern role for an urn set in a niche of a stone wall to catch the outpouring from a fountain mask. The water is designed to drain out of a hole in the base of the pitcher, to be recirculated into the fountain head. All the pipework has been cleverly hidden by planting. The noise from even the simplest of fountains is an added pleasure in hot summer gardens, but you need to experiment with the height of the spray and the depth of the receptacle to get the sound exactly right.

used to present the garden at its best and freshest so that you see it always with new eyes. Marijke Heuff's imaginative pictures make all sorts of ordinary things look beautiful. Her attention to detail and the way that she looks at gardens provide an illustration of how to see things in a different light. Growing plants is an absorbing and delightful pastime, but finding ways of showing them off to best advantage is garden making, which adds another dimension to gardening.

Traditionally, plants demand meticulous presentation to be seen at their best. This means dead flower heads and leaves must be removed and tidied regularly. But sometimes the work involved is out of all proportion to the result. For those who lack the time for finely tuned horticulture everywhere, a well chosen ornament can save hours of labour. If a border is past its best and falling into seedy disarray, an empty but beautiful pot can sometimes stand in for flowers. The Ali Baba jars among the autumn leaves on page 52 need nothing planted in or around them to attract attention. Anyone who has enjoyed the simple effects of gardens where flowers play a minor role will need no persuading that green and stone and water and air can make as much of a contribution to the garden as any border full of rarest flowers.

To some, the title of this book might suggest a superficial approach, but there is a twist in the wording: to 'decorate' can also suggest that you are giving a medal, a stamp of approval to what you see, and in a way that is what this book is all about. If it works, it should free garden makers from the confines of traditional taste and allow them to decorate their gardens with the stamp of their own approval, not with what others have suggested for them.

TOP AND ABOVE Simple fencing
contains dahlias, but the willows
are surrounded by a woven pal-
isade of their own branches – a
green version of basket-edging in
ironwork, popular in the early
nineteenth century.
LEFT A basin of water like a small
dew pond makes a centre for a
large display of plants dominated
by a giant tear-drop of yew.

*Seats capture the walker in a green no-man's land: here, where
petals fall and tendrils twine, you feel if you stayed for long enough
you might even become part of the garden.*

Garden Furniture

Garden furniture should be beautiful as well as useful. The seat where you relax has a dual function, for when it ceases to be a seat it becomes a part of the view. Set at the end of a path, it will be the focus of attention in its chosen resting place until you turn your back on it to sit down, so shape, size, colour and setting are all important. In the house, the choice is governed by whether a piece will 'go' with the room; out of doors the constraints are no less demanding. If the style is all spiky plants and sharp colours, benches and tables should be chosen to match, but traditional gardeners will tend to prefer old-fashioned patterns, in shades of blue and green or natural tones, to maintain an illusion of settled calm.

LEFT AND ABOVE The craftsmanship in a Chinese Chippendale-style chair deserves to be the focus of a special place. Humphry Repton, the famous landscape gardener of the eighteenth and early nineteenth centuries, favoured a similar blue to this for garden furniture because it goes well with greenery. The wheelbarrow bench, also in blue, is a good idea for gardeners who enjoy a change of scene.

Sitting down in a garden changes the perspective. Features that were a moment ago waist-high, now appear at eye-level. Plants become three-dimensional as you look straight into them, and even the dullest border is improved if you can arrange to gaze along its length at flower height. Seats capture the walker in a green no-man's land: here, where petals fall and tendrils twine, you feel if you stayed for long enough you might even become part of the garden. For those who enjoy intimations of immortality the garden seat is a place to dwell on eternal truths.

The pause for solitary reflection is one way of using a resting place in the garden. In another mood, somewhere for people to linger would demand a setting that had an enclosed and comfortable feeling, rather than one that encouraged timeless thoughts. The place where you sit for a meal or a drink needs to be near the house and a part of everyday domestic life. Here, comfort is more important than in other parts of the garden, and single chairs are often better than conventional benches. A chair can easily be moved up to the

table or into the shade, so it is a more tempting proposition than a heavy seat. When people sit down in twos and threes, each one sub-consciously sizes up the position of the chair and registers whether it can be shifted to suit their need. The more flexible you make this sort of arrangement, the more inviting it will seem.

Garden furniture can be bought in wood, canvas, wicker, metal or stone. Well-made hardwood chairs or benches with sloping backs always look right out of doors, but where space is short – and winters wet – wood has its drawbacks. Bad weather shortens the life of this most traditional of materials and it is better to store furniture inside than leave it out all year to face the elements. Where there is no room for bulky items, furniture such as deck chairs, directors' chairs of can-vas and wood or French café chairs in unassuming slats can be folded up at the end of summer. Like hardwood furniture, these merge natu-rally into the garden. Wicker, too, is easy to place, but not ideal where storage is in short supply.

If there is no room at all to keep furniture under cover, metal and stone are the best choice. Iron seats can look formal and uninviting, although old-fashioned balloon strapwork chairs are surprisingly com-fortable. Cheaper and lighter, aluminium is a good substitute for iron, but in elaborate patterns the detail is sometimes poor. Simple stone seats can be lovely, but in small gardens the weight and price of stone makes it perhaps the least suitable of all materials to choose.

LEFT AND FAR LEFT Benches are places for perching on. They are the kind of seats that people choose when they want to contemplate universal truths. Thoughts about life and death come easily under the dropping petals of a magnolia. Here, where the flowers fall, time passes, timelessly. For although a garden seems to be a place where time stands still, the passing of the seasons and the constant change and decay in nature underline a greater timescale than the wrist-watch or clock. Even the smallest garden needs a place for solitary musing. A corner dedicated to peace has an atmosphere that will be remembered long after the image of bright flowers has faded. In an increasingly developed world everyone needs somewhere to pause – call it peace or communing with nature. The simple wooden bench around the base of a tree is not perhaps the most comfortable of arrangements, but it allows the sitter whose aim is to be close to nature to lean against the trunk. If touching trees sounds like cranky therapy, try it and see how calming it is. Benches around trees should not be made too close to the trunk because the tree will need room to grow. Expensive hardwoods, which last for half a century and more, are usually the first choice for seats that are left out all year round. But if the seat is going to be close enough to the trunk to lean your back against it, it may be worth considering painted softwoods, so that they can be replaced within a couple of decades as the tree trunk expands.

RIGHT Moving large pieces of timber when trees have been felled can be expensive. One solution is to leave them where they fall and use them as seats. This log seems to have been taken over by nasturtiums and the prickly milk thistle, but with a little clearing of the area around, so that the thistle is no longer within reach, it would make a comfortable perch above the strawberries.

BELOW Two senior citizens among chairs are placed to catch the early spring sunshine, with the daffodils. The blue paint, even if battered, is the best of outdoor colours.

OPPOSITE The delightful iron chair (above), with its slatted wooden back and table for one, is an invitation to a drink at dusk among the evening primroses. The equally inviting but rather more sociable arrangement below illustrates how unimportant it is to have matching sets of furniture out of doors. A friendlier setting under the climbing rose and among the hardy geraniums and the froth of alchemilla could hardly be devised. Since sun tanning has been declared a health risk, shady bowers like this are essential. Few would wish to sit in the midday sun when they could be enjoying an *alfresco* meal here.

RIGHT For this spiky setting, where red hot pokers and sunset colours prevail, the park-bench type of seat with a thin arbour behind is a prosaic but practical choice. Slatted benches are useful pieces of furniture and because their backs slope they are often very comfortable – though their lack of arms at either end can make them seem unwelcoming. A more angular arrangement might have played up the demands of the planting scheme, or a solid piece of stone might have provided a contrast to all those vertical lines; rattan could perhaps make the place feel more exotic.

Sitting Outside

Sitting and thinking is all very well; but sometimes food for thought is not enough. Tables and chairs for real meals also have an important place in the garden. Sitting outside among family or friends, with a cup of coffee or a glass of wine, makes a garden belong to its owners. Used as an extra living room, it becomes a place that offers more attractions than flowers alone. A sitting place in the open air can also help to change the feelings of those for whom gardening is a chore. When a garden becomes associated with pleasure and relaxation, and ceases to be seen as a perpetual challenge, it may begin to appear more desirable.

The simple French café chairs used around two of these tables are among the cheapest available (left and opposite above). They

pack up flat for winter and can be painted in any colour. Dark green, grey-blue or brown are colours to choose if you want them to disappear; white makes them more noticeable. The tables themselves can be of the most improvised sort and, as here (left), a piece of slate or marble can be put on brick, stone or iron supports. An old softwood table can be covered with a plastic cloth to prolong its life (opposite above). An alternative would be to varnish it and leave it to get wet. (The best wooden tables are made of slatted hardwood, but these are rarely cheap.)

Being a natural material, wicker fits easily into an out-of-doors arrangement (right and far right). Chairs made from cane or rattan tend to be more comfortable than wooden ones, but they are not a good choice if there is nowhere to store them in long wet periods, as they will very quickly rot.

PREVIOUS PAGE Set amidst an ephemeral surge of colour, these French café chairs demonstrate their adaptability. Because they are portable and unobtrusive they can be moved from place to place to take advantage of the moment. When this border is past its best – when the red astilbes and tawny daylilies are over and the peppery smell of the pink phlox has begun to fade – it will be time to move on.

ABOVE Chairs made of branches or rustic wood can be restrained or sub-dued, like the pair under the win-dow that sit so demurely between the hostas. Alternatively they can branch out like the twisty monster on the left. This is the sort of cre-ation that might cause nightmares. These contorted windings could, you feel, like a wood in an Arthur Rackham illustration, soon turn into a threat. Here the grotesque is car-ried to extremes; but for those who like the idea of sitting down, per-haps never to rise again from a prison of tanglewood, it might be a dream, not a nightmare.

OPPOSITE ABOVE A delightful sofa has been crafted out of box, with a simple wooden seat; here box-green cushions might add to the picture of comfort. This could be a good place to create a living cushion of turf or camomile, in a raised bed retained by a wall of bricks or railway sleepers. Thyme looks lovely too, but beware of bees when sitting down.

OPPOSITE BELOW Gothic and rather grotesque, three chairs round a small wooden table are each cleverly carved out of one piece of wood. Chain saws, in care-ful hands, can create ingenious seats out of fallen tree trunks.

Eye-catchers

Seats are good eye-stoppers. Placed at the end of a path, as these three different benches have been, they provide a focus to walk towards. In large gardens, statues are often used to close a vista, but seats, with their dual function of ornament and useful object, may have the edge. The approach to a statue may be fine, but when you reach it the conclusion always seems, to me at least, rather unsatisfactory. Unless it is a Renaissance masterpiece that demands admiration of its detailed carving, there is not much you can do except stroke the stone (or composition concrete) and return the way you came.

With a seat, you can sit and look back at the path along which you have just walked and, if there are flowers on either side, you can enjoy them from a different angle. The scale changes too: even the purple cabbages will increase in size when you finally sit down on the blue ironwork seat and the human scale is halved (above left). The choice of wood for the seat at the end of the grass path through wild flowers is a happy one (left). A white seat, like the one framed under the arched supports spanning the herbaceous border, would have seemed too intrusive (above).

Beauty is in the eye of the beholder, and the garden is the place to express your own aesthetic.

Outdoor Art and Sculpture

The habit of ornamenting a garden came originally from Italy, where intricately carved urns and statues were chosen to be seen against a background of leaves and water. In smaller, flowerier places the plants provide the ornament, so what is needed is something much plainer to balance their distractions. This is why the green sculpture of topiary or hedges suits modern gardens so well. But where the planting is low-key, and the setting is peaceful, there is still a place for outdoor art. In art galleries the cry of 'I know what I like' may elicit a frosty response from the *cognoscenti*. But a private garden is the place to indulge in idiosyncratic preference and the belief that there is no such thing as absolute taste. Here beauty can be in the eye of the beholder, because unity is what matters. As long as the consistent vision of the owner governs the choice, it will be beautiful – sometimes, perhaps, only to one person, but gardens are essentially personal spaces where what you like is what counts. Eclectic art looks well displayed in a plain outdoor setting, and if after a time you tire of gnomes, old bicycle frames or cut-outs of goddesses, it should not cost too much to try something else. In the privacy of your own garden you can also try your hand at home-made art. As children, most of us could make or paint something and it is not beyond even the least gifted of adults to have a go at mosaic, a tablescape, or the placing of a funny or favourite object. Think of it as temporary, live with it for a while and see how it looks, add to it, change it and in the process you will learn about what you really do like and what your garden can take. This is a much more original way of approaching garden ornament than trying to adapt aspirational magazine pictures to less suitable surroundings. Which is not to say that all copying is a bad idea, but that it needs a spark of your own imagination if it is going to work for your private setting.

LEFT AND ABOVE Wood is the poor man's stone. Here, a home-made goddess Musica, cut out of plywood, sways baroquely on her plinth in the snow, while a decoy duck, with the air of a primitive carving, sails over a frosted wall. It is true that being exposed to winter will shorten the life of these objects, but it seems a pity to miss the chance to see them beautified by the snow.

Bought ornaments will always have a place in the garden, but those which mean something to the buyer are the ones that will continue to give pleasure long after their purchase. Animal lovers might enjoy putting representations of their favourites in unlikely places; bird fanciers could arrange to see a heron from the bedroom window every day; frustrated small-holders might be soothed by a stone bantam under an apple tree, or a cement pig behind the shed. And for those with traditional inclinations, a broken cherub or a cracked urn can often provide a more powerful image than a newly moulded reproduction. Association is brought into play here; if what you want to suggest is something of past grandeur, then moss and crumbling stonework will do this better than any copy of an ornament seen in an historic garden.

There are only two rules. The first is to stick to one theme, which means you should avoid mixing cherubs and discarded bicycles even if you love them both. The second is to find a way of making what you put in the garden particular to you, even if you cannot create it yourself. One of the greatest garden designers of recent times, Russell Page, was strict about what he called 'fancies and conceits' and liked to keep things simple from the start. But for those with less vision the only way of discovering what you don't like is to do it and then discard it when its magic has rubbed away.

ABOVE Stone statues tend to be out of the affordable bracket, but sometimes badly damaged pieces, like this cherub with a hat of succulents, are within the budget. Broken ornaments have an extra poignancy, underlining as they do the passage of time and the decay of everything. Cherubs can be sickly sweet, but this one is more endearing than annoying. And if the sight of armless statues dismays you, think of the *Venus de Milo*.

LEFT AND FAR LEFT Musica, covered in snow on page 26, is here seen at the end of a grassy vista. Despite her plywood origins, she looks not at all wooden because of the movement in the painted curves of her skirt. The pageboy among the fallen apples is also two-dimensional. Eighteenth-century gardeners recognized the tradition of theatricality out of doors, often using painted features like these. Gilbert White, the Hampshire vicar who kept a record of his observations of nature from 1751 until 1768, was a man of modest means, but, like the rest of his generation, felt a garden was incomplete without a statue; so he had a vista cut through hedges and at the end of this he placed a silhouette of Hercules on a painted board.

ABOVE For hobby artists, the garden offers a permanent exhibition setting for works that may have outgrown the home. Self-expression is quite in order out of doors. The potter who modelled these two clay buildings must have enjoyed placing them in sites worthy of them. The oriental-looking roof on the left has been given its own miniature jungle of finely cut leaves. The Indian-inspired pavilion (right), sits where it can gaze at its own reflection.

OPPOSITE The mosaic pigeon house is an ambitious structure, but the idea would not be difficult to copy. Pieces of china are stuck into a cement rendering before it hardens. This is work that may need more than one person if it is not to take forever, and if the cement is not to dry out before it is finished. It also needs careful planning of the pattern; a scale plan on graph paper is useful and it is probably a good idea to lay out the pattern on the ground in sections, so that it can be transferred from there to the walls. A complicated mosaic is not something to undertake without a sufficient supply of broken china that has been reduced to fragments of roughly the same size – running out of material in mid-project could jeopardize the rest of your crockery. In a good mosaic there should be more stone than setting. Small swimming-pool mosaic tiles might be worth trying for more refined work, provided the colours were good enough and there was enough variety in the shading.

Birds and Beasts

Quite undistinguished pieces of mass-produced wares can be transformed by clever placing. They may not bear close inspection, but from a distance the outline of a pig or a chicken, say, in an orchard – or a cat up a tree (below right) –should evoke an amused smile from the onlooker. The Victorians, who had a sentimental attitude to most things, were fond of putting life-size animals in the grass. This tradition is not unknown today: one modern tycoon with ecological leanings has a bronze rhinoceros in his London

orchard, and art-loving horse-fanciers put a Frink sculpture on the lawn. The domestic scale of animals makes them better subjects for sculpture in small gardens than gods and goddesses. If the dog on guard here (opposite below) had been one of a pair and both had been set on plinths on either side of the gate, the effect would have been imposing and perhaps less suitable for a modest setting. The bird poised by the water's edge (above) and the cat on the tree have both been placed for maximum pleasure. The painted tin sheep by the gate would not deceive anyone: like a caricature, it has been put there for a laugh (opposite right). Statues as small as these do not have to be stationary; the beauty of small ones is that they are easy to move. When what once seemed a whimsical touch begins to cloy, then a new place can be chosen: the cat can prowl in long grass and the toads (centre) can be banished to a shrubby

corner. In new settings, familiar faces take on another life, but when the first statue has been a success, the temptation to add another can be irresistible. This will, however, reduce the element of surprise: the eyeful of a cat up a tree, two dogs on guard at the gate, a couple of toads, a fowl and a sheep would then produce quite a different reaction.

ABOVE The golden cockerel on the gable of this simple building draws the eye upwards. Weathervanes are good ornaments to choose, because they also have a purpose. William Morris recommended that only those things that are beautiful or useful should be included in a room, which is not a bad rule for a garden. If both qualities can be combined, as they are here, it is easy to justify some adornment. Sundials are another example of useful and decorative objects for gardeners who like to know the time of day as well as which way the wind is blowing. Weathervanes are probably easier than sundials to make at home, as they can be cut out of a piece of flat tin and painted. The base of a large biscuit tin might not make a cockerel as flamboyant as this, but it should be enough for a simple arrow to point into the wind. Ambitious carpenters might like to try making a weathervane out of plywood, which can be painted with yacht paint and then varnished.

ABOVE Gnomes, though certainly not useful, are beautiful to some. German rock gardens had gnomes in them in the eighteenth century; in England in the latter half of the nineteenth century they began to appear in the rockeries of grand gardens. Like all fashions, they started out as exclusive and gradually became more popular. (William Morris and Gertrude Jekyll, high priests of the Arts and Crafts movement in gardening, were not in favour of gnomes.) In this century the mass appeal of gnomes has turned them into kitsch items: they do not appear in the best gardens. When you look at these creatures, so lovingly placed under the canopy of a blue fir, their owner's delight is unmistakable. Hand-made pottery gnomes modelled by children and painted with affection might be hard to resist out of doors. The less image-conscious can continue to buy the large numbers of gnomes that are still being made and have fun putting them in the perfect place.

Mirror Images

Reflections are desirable things in any garden, heightening sensa-
tions and creating unexpected impressions. Sometimes, where there
is no room for water, a mirage does the trick equally well. On the
Continent, silver balls, like Christmas tree decorations, are tradi-
tionally used to keep evil spirits at bay, while also acting as mir-
rors. Here, among the greenery, a golden image of a building is
caught in a bowl of reflection (right). Mirrors can also be used out-
side, not to simulate water but to give an illusion of depth. At the
end of the trellis tunnel, a looking-glass has been placed to make it
seem that the green passage is much longer than it really is (above).
Only the bird, with its reflection caught in the glass, gives the game

away. Those who are tempted by this trick may find that a piece of old glass looks less obvious than a brand new one destined for a bathroom fitting.

Real water will reflect if it does not have too many plants growing in or on it. A floating clear glass ball creates a transparent bubble, which provides the reflection that the lily-covered pond will not now give (above).

Displays and Collections

*Creative work is not everyone's style but arranging things is within
most people's range. There are plenty of organic objects which can
be organized into arrangements that are as beautiful as works of
art. The Christmas tree hung with apples and nuts (above) is
strictly for the birds, but it is also a visual surprise for humankind.
Natural phenomena are taken for granted in their ordinary settings. Few people stop to admire a seed pot or row of growing lettuces, but pack the seeds into a box, or put the lettuces in a basket,
and the reaction is quite different. Seeds and fruits set out in com-
partments (right) look much more arresting in a mass than they*

would individually. Because seeds are small they tend to look unremarkable in nature and their variety is never appreciated, as it can be when they are seen all together. Fungi, too, have all the fascination of the unfamiliar when they are grouped into a display, as they are here (top). Arrangements like these are temporary, but like the heaps of scrubbed vegetables at a horticultural show, they provide a spectacle. Presentation is the key to making people take a second look at ordinary objects, and a tablescape of even such humble things as stones (above) gives them the dignity of collectors' pieces.

Pots, like urns, make any plant seem special. Less expensive than stoneware statuary and lighter to move around, they can be used on paving or amidst borders for changing displays of flowers.

Pots and Containers

Pots are the economical gardener's answer to urns and vases. Their scale and substance, too, is often more appropriate in small gardens than large copies of ornaments that were designed for grander

places. Traditionally pots are made of terracotta and if they are to stand outside in winter they need to be fired at high temperatures, so the strongest pots will be those made from the reddest clay. Ornaments of hot orange can look alien in areas where stone, rather than brick, is the dominant building material, but there are ways of avoiding this clash. Vita Sackville-West recommended a coat of whitewash – a lime distemper, that is, not a stark white impervious masonry paint – for fiercely coloured pots, which is still worth trying. If you want to go further and make the pots look like stone, a little raw umber can be mixed into the whitewash solution.

LEFT AND ABOVE Auriculas need to be seen at close quarters to be appreciated. Here, set into a wicker basket and placed on a chair, it is hard to ignore them. A single bergenia in a pot, put in a place where you might trip over it, might be a bit of an anticlimax, but this regular row of juvenile plants on the wall is a reassuring sight.

Clay pots coloured with blue or green glazes, or very dark brown if from a traditional kiln, can all look good in certain settings. Pale clays will be more likely to crack in the frost than the darker ones. All pots need to be placed where water can drain away in winter; waterlogged containers that freeze have a high risk of cracking. Set the pots on stones, or feet of clay, a couple of inches above the ground, but if the pot is valuable, empty it and bring it inside for winter.

In Mediterranean countries empty engine oil cans, old olive tins, buckets and other unlikely containers are pressed into service as pots for growing geraniums, basil and other plants. Sometimes they are painted bright blue or green and their random heights and sizes make for interesting groups around doorsteps and on balconies. An assortment of shapes is a good idea, but it is usually more effective to use simple, useful containers which do not compete with the plants for attention. A well-grown geranium flowering in an old tin or a wooden tub will attract the eye to the flower, but a ring of busy Lizzies set in a car tyre or a wheelbarrow will draw attention to the unusual container, rather than the plants – which is fine if you wish to be congratulated on your ability to recycle old materials, but less good if your aim is to show off flowers.

Pot-grown plants can be put into groups of single sorts, or they can be combined in one large pot. The current English fashion for cramming large garden pots with a variety of rare and tender bedding is the gardener's equivalent of high floristry. Flowering pots with a central foliage plant of a cordyline, yucca or canna, with cascades of flowers in associated colours are, to me, the outdoor version of the triangular, oasis-bound flower bouquet. Just as simple containers indoors can look

ABOVE The white wirework stand holding scarlet petunias makes a showy group for a town garden. Like unexpected settings, isolated colour ranges attract attention. Compare this with the complementary greens of plant tray and shutters, opposite, to see which effect you prefer for bright reds.

good with less ambitious arrangements, so it can sometimes be pretentious in a small garden to go overboard on the pots. In some positions one large container looks terrific, but where the scale is more domestic, on either side of a door or on steps for example, it may be more effective to keep plants in separate smaller pots and build up groups in different colour schemes.

ABOVE Red and orange begonias in an alternative version of a window-box, which is no more than an iron grille hanging below the window, with a green plastic tray to hold the pots. Window-boxes must be safely anchored if they are not to be dangerous, and this looks like a good, as well as an attractive, system.

RIGHT, TOP Here the red and green of the coleus leaves against terracotta and green of pot and shutters makes an irresistible colour scheme, if in a rather precarious position. Like holly with its berries, the shades are complementary, that is, they are opposite each other on the colour wheel.

ABOVE Strongly coloured bedding plants can be indigestible in a mass, but grown in pots, such as these zinnias and marigolds, they can be used to advantage around the garden in summer. They may be too brash for dull areas, but can be a good way to liven up utilitarian areas such as around a cold frame.

Wooden tubs make simple and cheap containers, but it is important to ensure that they have not been creosoted before they are planted, as this treatment can be lethal to plant life. Because they are deep, they need a large amount of soil, and if this is not to come out of the garden it will be an expensive purchase. A scatter of crocks in the bottom, topped with a layer of crumpled balls of newspaper can reduce the quantity of soil needed. Newspaper is a good moisture retainer and, if there is no tap near large containers, this trick can also help to cut down the time spent watering.

Foxgloves are adaptable plants for containers, because they respond well to being moved at any stage of their lives. They could be used to fill the awkward gap between spring bulbs and summer bedding. For large containers like these, tall plants are vital. Ideally the plants should represent two-thirds, to the tub's one third, of the overall height; otherwise the proportions can look mean. Finding large enough plants throughout the seasons can be a problem. The solution may be to stick to something that is dramatic all year round, like *Euphorbia characias* ssp. *wulfenii*.

OPPOSITE Old coppers, which were formerly used to boil the family wash, can still be bought in Europe not too expensively – a lovely example occupies the centre of the Cottage Garden at Sissinghurst, Kent. It seems a pity not to reveal the verdigris sides of such paupers' antiques, and this crowd of daisies hardly needs its supporting cast of extras around the base.

BELOW When containers are broader than they are high, low-growing plants do not look so out of proportion as they might in tall, narrow-planters. Set amidst a flowerbed, this large, shallow bowl is mass-planted with tiny violas, visible above the flower heads of a carpet of ajuga.

LEFT AND BELOW Tall pots with narrow necks are awkward to plant but the amphora shape (left) is beautiful enough to stand on its own. The strawberries in the pot (below left) may distort its shape, but they look so agreeable emerging from all sides that it hardly matters. The datura in the plain wooden tub (below right) would also have been a good choice for a narrow-necked pot, provided it was not left there for too long, because extracting established roots from the neck of a precious terracotta pot is difficult. A simple trolley would be needed to move a planted pot or tub of this size under cover for winter.

TOP The 'stone' sinks standing in a little concrete yard are an inspired example of how to treat a difficult corner on a low budget. Some are old discarded china sinks, coated in a mixture of sand, peat and cement; others are made in reconstituted stone.

ABOVE Plastic is not always a desirable medium for ornament in a garden, but these oblong seedboxes, arranged in a wheel around a tree, make a lovely pattern.

RIGHT Pans of alpines occupy a set of steps outside a shed. Tiered staging is often used to show off plants, and is the perfect means of presenting small specimens. For me, however, the tumbling cascade of ivy breaks the orderliness of the succulents and stonecrops. They have their own appeal, and it is perhaps a different one to that of a fall of ivy. Mixing styles of plant is sometimes exciting, it depends on what you want to emphasize.

ABOVE Empty terracotta pots waiting tidily to be planted have the peculiar charm of a good tool in the right place.

Restrained Planting

'Sameness is all' wrote the great modern landscape architect, Nan Fairbrother. If it is not very well done, the recent fashion for planting pots with seven or eight varieties of plants can be visually exhausting. Sometimes it can be more compelling – as well as much easier to maintain – if a group of pots is all planted alike. The row of half pots all filled with lavender (right) may not look horticulturally challenging, but the effect is well planned and orderly. In gardens where time is short, this may be a simpler way of treating pots than more ambitious schemes. Pot-grown plants need to be rigorously maintained, which means daily dead-heading and watering, as well as weekly liquid feeding. Water-retaining gel granules can now be bought to mix into the soil, thereby reducing the need to

water so often in dry weather. These horticultural 'polymers' are not infallible because rain can swell the granules to make pots unacceptably wet, so they need to be used carefully.

Simplicity is also a good idea in small gardens where exuberant plantings in the flower beds can exhaust the eye. Topiary balls on either side of a door (left) may not look quite as much fun as a cornucopia of summer colour, but after a rich diet of flowers they provide a welcome rest. In winter, evergreens really come into their own. When the border of grasses has died down behind the terrace (far right), the lead boxes of ivy will still be there to see. It is tempting to go all out for sensation, but restraint in a garden is refreshing. The stone bench with two simple pots of busy Lizzies is a beautiful object (right); cluttered with mixed flowers, this simple effect would be lost.

ABOVE Pots in different materials are enhanced by colours which complement their own. If the containers are good enough, they can even be left unplanted, as these Ali Baba jars have been. Standing under a flame-coloured acer among fallen leaves, their terracotta presence improves an autumn picture.
RIGHT Green plants enliven stone better than blue ones. The stone trough in this picture, filled with purple violas, looks cheerful next to the greenery on the right, and sober near the blue hostas on the left. The hostas are, however, a particularly good colour contrast to the bricks in the wall.

BELOW LEFT The blue-grey of galvanized iron is echoed in the colouring of lavender and sage. Yellow flowers would add a note of sophistication. Any tin or bucket originally intended to hold water, or indeed any container not destined from the start for the growing of plants, needs to be drilled for drainage holes; some stone troughs must also be made to drain properly. For Mediterranean plants, most herbs – including those shown here – and all alpines, good drainage is critical.

BELOW Setting a pot on a plinth makes it special, particularly if the plant can act as a visual centrepiece – such as this *Heuchera micrantha* 'Palace Purple'.

BOTTOM A collection of pots around a solid central feature like a full-size barrel or disused water butt can make a strong group in a place where flowerbeds are impossible or past their seasonal best. Lilies make a good display here: they are best in deep containers like these, and will also do well in shade.

Where statues or stone vases are unaffordable, trees and shrubs can be manufactured into living sculpture. Their regular outlines are a solid presence in a changing garden.

Green Sculpture

Green sculpture turns plants from a natural shape into one of the gardener's choosing. In formal gardens, even the plants are expected to conform. Trees that might seem unwieldy in small spaces can be trained to grow horizontally, like flat one-dimensional cut-outs. Espaliered or pleached, their branches are tamed to provide strong, straight lines wherever they are needed. Once pleaching was used in large formal gardens for avenues; now it becomes a way to create parallel lines in the air for those who measure their plots in square metres rather than acres. Hedges on stilts are carved slices of green above a tumble of flowers. Trees (and shrubs) can also be sculpted in the round. Grown as standards, like huge lollipops on sticks, specimens that might be too big or informal for small spaces become easy to manage and can be kept in scale with their surroundings. Their regular outlines are a solid presence in a changing garden. Where statues or stone vases are unaffordable, trees and shrubs can be manufactured into living sculpture.

LEFT AND ABOVE It is interesting to compare the differences between subjects cut from yew and those from box. The box creatures look livelier because their glossy leaves reflect the light, but the oversize yew bird echoing the shape of the thatched porch is certainly more monumental.

Topiary takes green sculpture a stage further, to the brink of fantasy and beyond. Coaxing a shape from a bush of yew or box has always been a speciality of the cottage gardener, who devoted years of patience and skill to this art. In small gardens the tradition of topiary continues to thrive as a means of self-expression. It remains the best way of adding substance to a planting, while indulging in a bit of DIY sculpture. Topiary shapes can be formal, informal, abstract, witty, scary, beautiful or mad – whatever fits the mood of the garden. For those who lack the confidence with shears, there are frames in light aluminium that sketch in the ultimate outline, while providing a guideline for the clipper. And for those short on patience, ivy can be grown into and over the frames in a relatively short space of time.

Early topiary was cut from quickthorn (hawthorn) and there are plenty of shrubs that will respond to repeated cutting, but those with small leaves will always make the best specimens. It seems a pity, however, to use deciduous plants when evergreens will adorn a garden all year round. For the impatient, *Lonicera nitida* will grow fast, but it will need clipping four or five times a year to keep it in shape. Glossy box is difficult for detailed work, but it is a good plant for the strong abstract shapes of balls or spirals. Best of all is the dense and dark yew, which can be turned into almost any angle or curve. It is slow growing, but can with encouragement put on about 20 cm (8 in) a year. Ultimately, plants that are naturally slow, like box and yew, are the best ones to choose because they will need less maintenance.

When plants are being thwarted of their natural habit of growth they need plenty of encouragement. Constant cutting makes intensive demands, and compensation in the form of extra rations and water in dry conditions will always be important. If this sounds like hard work, there are alternatives. Some plants naturally grow into regular shapes and although these will never look as crisp and strong as those that are clipped and shaped to order, they are worth considering where time is short. New box hybrids can be found that will grow into fastigiate or dome shapes. Some plants like santolinas, hebes and potentillas form natural hummocks of dense foliage, and others like junipers, Irish yews, poplars and hornbeams can all be chosen in upright forms.

RIGHT The contorted forms of pleached limes demonstrate a different way of shaping plants. Here the trees have been pruned to leave a framework of extended branches, which is more clearly shown in the emerging leaves below, than in the summer greenery above. The curling tracery here looks more exciting than traditional pleaching, because the branches curve upwards, as they naturally like to do. Where trees need to be severely pleached, the shoots are tied along horizontal wires, supported on stout posts. Limes of the common European form often produce a mass of suckers at the base of their trunks, but Dutch-grown forms seem to be less susceptible. All European limes are variable, so when the trees are designed for a formal scheme it is important to insist on plants that have been raised from cuttings taken from the same stock plant.

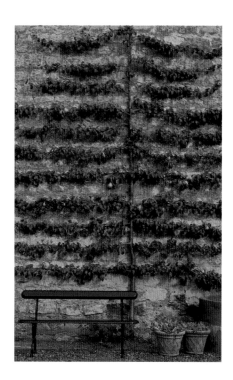

ABOVE The same principles of training are here applied to a pear tree grown against a wall. This method, known as espalier, can also be done like pleaching on a free-standing arrangement of posts and wires. Once the framework has been developed, pruning is simple and consists of cutting back the side shoots that grow from the main lateral branches. This can be performed in winter, which increases vigour, and again in summer to restrict growth.

ABOVE Apples and pears are among the most obliging of plants for green sculpture. Here apples have been trained into a version of a goblet, each arm supported with a bamboo stick. As with espaliers, when the trees reach the right height the branches need to be stopped and the side shoots regularly trimmed back to encourage fruit production. On young plants, it is better to remove the flower buds to prevent any fruit from forming, so that the tree can develop a sturdy framework.

RIGHT Ivy is an adaptable plant for quick and easy effect. This golden-leaved snake trained on strong wire will cover its support in a couple of years, when it can be clipped to maintain the spiral shape.

OPPOSITE ABOVE Box is being trained to grow into an elegant, Empire-style sofa, with the help of iron and stone.

NEAR RIGHT Buttresses of golden privet surround a porch; where no porch exists, green sculpture might furnish one.

FAR RIGHT The ultimate in garden designer furniture is the bay with a twisted stem. These specimens are very expensive to buy, but for those who like their curves baroque, they are possible to grow. Like standards, they take time and it should also be remembered that bay is not hardy in cold zones, so your tree will need to be moved indoors in winter. To create this barley-sugar twist, the young stem is gradually turned around a central support.

TOP Santolina, or cotton lavender, was popular in Elizabethan times for clipped work. Here the grey domes have been allowed to keep their yellow flowers, which are sometimes removed in formal schemes. Santolina is not reliably hardy and can disappear in cold winters; it also has the disadvantage of looking bare and twiggy when it is given its annual trim, which should be done after all danger of hard frost has passed. In cold, heavy, waterlogged soils it will probably not survive the winter.

ABOVE Box balls are crisper in outline than santolina, so they tend to be used for formal gestures. But here, the group of huddled, round bushes look like an organic sculpture. A sea of stylized waves, a heap of honeycomb, a flock of sheep – the rounded shapes suggest plenty of images. Cutting these must be very testing as there is barely an inch of space between the bushes.

ABOVE AND LEFT The potted bushes (above) are in a different mood – neat, man-made full stops to be placed wherever the eye needs a rest. Clipped shapes like these suggest control. The large box balls on sentry duty along the path (left) are less severely effective as full stops, because plants are creeping out from under the bushes over the path. This broken symmetry may be just what the owner intended, with anarchy perhaps not too far behind.

Standard Shapes

Standard trees like lollipops on sticks are useful in small gardens, because they provide height without casting too much shade. This way of growing plants also means that many types can be chosen that might otherwise be too large. Some flowering viburnums naturally make big bushes, which might disqualify their presence in

small gardens. Grown as standards (left), their flowers can be smelt and admired in spring; for the rest of the year, instead of a large dull bush, there will be two neat trees of green above the flowers. The hollies above cut squares of yew (right) would also have been too large in their natural form, and the weeping mulberries with their shaggy haircut (below) can be an untidy sight when grown more freely. Ivies will not make self-supporting lollipops, but trained up a frame they will oblige by growing quickly into trees (below right).

Standards tend to be expensive to buy, because although they are not difficult, it can be a slow business producing a fully developed example. Patient gardeners can grow standards for a pittance. For the first few years a single shoot should be selected and trained to a

stout cane. This can be allowed to make a few shoots and leaves out from the main stem, but when the trunk reaches the desired height and the tip is nipped off, the side shoots on the trunk must be pruned away. As the top branches start to grow, they too are pinched back, so that a sturdy head is developed. In four or five years, the little tree should be a good shape. Impatient gardeners can make standards of redcurrants, gooseberries, fuchsias and pelargoniums: lilacs and evergreens take longer. For a standard rose, try taking cuttings in late summer from a strong climber or large shrub rose, and training it as above. Within three years, if well fed and watered, you should have a supported standard growing on its own roots. Small-flowered varieties, like 'Sanders' White Rambler' or 'Ballerina,' are most suitable.

ABOVE Several strong shapes compete for attention in this picture. At the back are two standard golden conifers with various chess-men and balls of box at their feet. The shuttlecock fern, like poised angels' wings, can be seen between the conifers. The impact created by each of these features – which on their own would have provided a solid green space at the heart of a flowery riot – is stimulating rather than restful.

RIGHT Herb gardens can be hard to manage, because herbs have a habit of dying out in wet winters and many of the aromatic sun-lovers are not long-lived. Hedges of thyme, lavender and rue can be unreliable in cold climates, so box is often the safest bet for edging. A ring of artemisia is an alternative as a change from box, but might be more troublesome to keep up. The roots are prone to running, so that shoots come up everywhere, widening and distorting the hedge; the plant also needs to be cut back hard in late spring if it is not to become woody at its base.

ABOVE AND RIGHT The clipping of box varies in every garden. Around the herbs (left) it can be seen sheered to precision, with a level top and flat sides; but in these two small curving parterres, the hedges are rounded and fluffy. In the United States, and particularly in Virginia, there is a tradition of plucking, rather than cutting, box, which gives it this softer look. It is worth visiting a specialist box nursery for advice on which of the many forms to grow. In addition to the well-known dwarf edging box (*Buxus suffruticosa*), there are varieties which naturally grow into domed or upright shapes. Some are faster than others, and leaf size and shape varies.

RIGHT AND BELOW The art of topiary cut free-hand is centuries old. In early English gardens topiary was usually made from box; later, yew became popular. The primitive bird on the obelisk is made of yew, but the pair of birds flanking the cottage entrance are shaped from privet, a semi-evergreen that grows more quickly than either yew or box. Because of its speed of growth, it needs clipping more often: four or five cuts per year would only just be enough to keep the birds looking as trim as they do here. Yew and box, when fully grown, need only one cut a year in late summer, but all topiary needs regular feeding.

LEFT AND FAR LEFT For more ambitious green sculptures, frames can now be bought, like this skeleton of a horse that is beginning to be fleshed out with ivy. The body has been covered with chicken wire, but it could be filled with crumpled newspaper and covered with a thick layer of moss; either method would give the ivy something to cling to, and prevent it from wasting too much of its growth inside the horse. The moose cut from golden privet is a creature in the best heraldic tradition. His antlers would need to be trained to a hoop of wire, but the rest of his body could probably be cut freestyle.

Garden visitors tend to see plants either as drifts of colour or as flower faces, to be studied close-up like a botanical illustration. But some plants stand out from the crowd and are best when seen alone.

Plants in Focus

Vegetable sculpture is art for the outdoor room. We may rely on topiary for the permanent display, but there are plenty of plants to be used for temporary effects. It makes them more exciting if they can be made to appear and disappear at will. Topiary grows imperceptibly and gives a garden a settled atmosphere. For instant drama, the Jack-and-the-beanstalk plants are the ones to use; some will make as much as two metres of growth in a season. Like giant exclamation marks, silver thistles, green angelica and woodland tobacco plants will all grow in a summer to a colossal size. Other verticals on a smaller scale, like foxgloves, mulleins, delphiniums and hollyhocks, also have the effect of making the eye travel up and down their height. Normally we scan a flower bed from side to side, so anything that changes that emphasis creates a pause for the viewer and breaks a dull routine.

LEFT The woolly mullein makes an impressive sight in any bed. Here it towers over its smaller relations as well as the bold outlines of the surrounding ferns. ABOVE Red valerian growing around a garden seat will be in flower for most of the summer. Seeding happily in cracks of brick and stone, it needs little attention, but deadheading keeps it going for longer.

Some plants can be arresting, not because of their height but for their shape. Those with leaves that make bold outlines can give substance to plantings or be used as features on their own. In a place that seems to call for a large pot, a figure or a seat, sometimes a plant will fill the gap. It might be a tree with elegant boughs, like the ordinary *Magnolia* x *soulangeana* with its distinctive shape, like *Viburnum plicatum* 'Llanarth' with its flat tiers of branches, or perhaps a plant with swords for leaves, like a yucca or a grand *Crocosmia*. Statuesque stands of large well-defined leaves – gunnera, ferns, acanthus, hostas, brunnera, peonies – are always impressive. The secret is to use these strong leaves sparingly: when they compete with one another for attention, the impact is reduced.

A concentration of colour can also be a feature that stands out in a garden, so that what is noticed first is not the individual flowers, but the overall effect. This sort of gardening has got itself a bad name, because gardeners who care more for a splash of colour than for growing rare and difficult plants are not much admired now. Like all popular and simple effects this is one of the hardest to stage. A single meconopsis, with its bluest of blue poppy flowers, is a rarity but a whole patch of meconopsis will excite not just the connoisseur, but the lover of beauty as well. With less rare plants, growing more of them enhances their image. Even quite a dull plant like valerian, which seeds itself everywhere, can be lovely when massed. In a flower bed, the pink flower heads would never excite much interest, but clinging to the face of a stone wall, valerian looks quite different. There are all sorts of other flowers that get taken for granted (aquilegias, forget-me-nots, foxgloves or yellow Welsh poppies), but if they are allowed to seed through a garden so that they appear to have colonized it, they will become a feature of that garden. And if you are lucky enough to have one of these prodigals for each season of the year, their generous presence will give the place a unity that cannot be arranged by grouping carefully chosen rarities. Allowing common plants to repeat themselves in borders and shrubberies, and even in paths, makes a garden feel like a place where plants are always happy.

ABOVE, RIGHT AND OPPOSITE Some plants are arresting enough to stand on their own. The globe artichoke is the giant dwarfing the round grey bushes of santolina (right, top). More usually seen as an impressive foliage plant for the large border, here the low box hedges turn it into an absurd horticultural joke. Similarly boxed in, the giant crambe (right) is a wonderful sight anywhere in the garden with its foaming sprays of flowers in early summer. After flowering, the leaves can get tatty if the spikes are not removed before they seed, and those who want more in their garden than one spectacular flowering will have to devise a replacement: the tall, airy *Verbena bonariensis*, a late summer feature, might make a good follow-up if it was planted *en masse* around the crambe. The prickly agave (opposite, top), masquerading as a piece of stone work, has no need of flowers. This is a plant you either love or hate for its dramatic architectural habit.

ABOVE AND NEAR RIGHT
Gardeners divide into two camps:
those who seek the distractions of
variety and those who opt for a
singular beauty. In small gardens
simple effects are often the most
successful. A band of beautifully
grown pink and white annual mal-
lows (above) might give more pleasure than a collection of rare
plants. They will also be easier to
manage. Those who are lucky
enough to be able to grow the
Himalayan blue poppy (near right)
can indulge in an enviable display.
Although both the poppies and the
rhododendrons will be over in a
matter of weeks, their impact is so
stunning that on acid soil in shady
places it is worth sacrificing the
space to this late spring coup.

FAR RIGHT Spring bulbs are tempting and it always seems a pity not to
grow all of them. But the restraint
shown in planting only two colours
of crocus around the tree (top)
refutes such self-indulgence. Other
single species plantings for spring –
snowdrops perhaps, or scillas, or
best of all cyclamen – can be equally
effective. The parrot tulips (bottom)
are for lovers of the baroque. They
are such flamboyant flowers that
to plant them in mean ones and
twos would curb their extravagant
spirit. Clumps of tulips (not rows),
among shrubs and plants that will
later come into their own, give a
spring splash of colour among
greenery. If possible, site them so
that their dying stems are concealed
by summer-performing plants.

OVERLEAF A June dawn, with
dew covering the grass and
mullein silhouettes among the
roses, casts a spell over this garden.
Even by day, their huge, silvery
leaves and lemon-yellow flowers
are a ghostly presence.

TOP Woodland plants around the wood-shed – honesty, ferns and for-get-me-not-blue brunnera – create the perfect low-key setting in light woodland. More gardening effort here, with flower beds or roses, would have struck a quite different, and much less appropriate, note. In spring, flowers will dominate, but as the leaf cover increases, the effect under these trees will be entirely green. The bold outlines of the ferns will continue to be a feature throughout the summer.

ABOVE Hollyhocks are traditional cottage plants, especially these single ones. Hollyhocks like plenty of sun and will thrive in dry soil, so a position against a house wall suits them particularly well. Where they are prone to rust, they should be grown and treated as biennials, but they will often seed themselves to save the gardener the trouble. (One of the few benefits of town gardening is that they do not seem to be so susceptible to rust in areas where air pollution is a problem.)

ABOVE Giant hogweed seen against this thatched and boarded building gives the place the look of a Grimm's fairy tale. This is a plant for lovers of the surreal and the fabulous. Like an outsize cow parsley, giant hogweed stalks the garden. But it has to come with a warning, because its sap can cause an allergic reaction in some people. It is also a prolific seeder, so unless you want an army of mammoth plants, it should be beheaded before it starts to spread. For anyone who wants a tropical or exotic feature, this is the plant to have, but for those who do not feel quite up to the demands of giant hogweed, a gunnera or angelica might be a less stressful choice. All of these monsters like moist soil best. Angelica is technically biennial, but if it can be prevented from setting seed it will often behave like a perennial.

Seeds and Fruits

Plants that have a second season are invaluable in small gardens, and sometimes their seedheads or fruits can be showier and last longer than the flowers. The round red hips of rugosa roses (below left) last until early winter. Alliums, with seedheads that look like bursts of fireworks (below centre), or the honeycombed balls of Scabiosa stellata (below right) will continue to dominate a border long after the flowers have faded, when their shapes come to count for more than their colours; but the familiar iceplant (right) has a further virtue, for it hangs on to its rust-red colour all through the winter.

The idea of letting some plants go to seed upsets tidy gardeners. Some plants like thistles and sweet Cicely, which can reproduce themselves anywhere, will take advantage of the relaxed routine that allows them to keep their seedheads and spread themselves around. But as one can never have enough of most of the plants with ornamental seeds, their progeny is usually a bonus. There are peonies with crimson and scarlet seed pods and honesty with silvery pennies. Then there are the plants with decorative fruits, such as common spindle with orange and pink berries, viburnums with wine red and yellow fruits – all are available just when the garden seems to be over for another year.

Those who want roses to be followed by hips (which will rarely occur on modern garden roses) should sacrifice a last crop of flowers as late summer approaches. Dead-heading the rugosas may encourage them to produce more blooms, but it also puts paid to their fruits.

There is a practical advantage for the gardener who uses seedheads to extend the season of interest. The annual autumn clean-up of borders practised by the orderly gardener is a heavy chore. The indulgent gardener not only has the winter pleasures of hoar frost on the skeletons of the plants, but in spring the stems that carry the seedheads are straw-light. What would have taken many hours to cut down and wheel away when green is the work of a few moments to clear in spring.

BELOW Large leaves of the rhubarb family create an exotic tropical effect. Just as vertical plants hold the eye as it registers the plant from top to bottom, these titans of the plant kingdom slow the eye down and make it scan from side to side.

BOTTOM Another exotic with fleshy leaves, *Eucomis* is known as the pineapple plant because of its tufts of leaves above greenish flowers. Other plants with lush leaves for jungle effects are the arum lilies, *Lysichiton*, *Veratrum* and fatsia.

LEFT Ruby chard is eye-catching enough to grow with the flowers. Other vegetables with arresting leaves are globe artichokes, purple cabbages and the continental frilly lettuces. A row of ruby spinach beet grown next to potatoes makes a cheerful contrast to their bland green tops, and a line of artichokes makes a good edge to any kitchen plot.

BELOW Acanthus leaves, the inspiration for the capitals of the temple at Corinth by Callimachus, are a classical ornament for modern gardeners. Here a line of acanthus grows in front of a wall whose colour underlines that of the curious hooded flowers. Acanthus, the easiest of plants to grow in sun or shade, will sometimes spread itself a little too enthusiastically, but in the right place it is a boon.

Ideas cost nothing. Using real objects to kick-start a train of thought was an eighteenth-century trick. In modern gardens quite ordinary things can be used to trigger associations.

Artless Art

LEFT AND ABOVE The bottomless boat is still beautiful with its curving sides of oak. Here is a place where children might spend hours in play, while the onlooker is reminded of happy summers on the river and the sadness of things that have seen better days. In contrast, the barrow-load of fruit and the chicken suggest the pleasures of self-sufficiency.

Much of garden-making is about illusion, and gardens, like stages, need props. In the best productions these cost money, but improvisation has a place in the theatre, as it does in the garden. Expensive statues are not *de rigueur* and reproductions of urns meant for formal gardens look pretentious in smaller places. Even the most ordinary objects rate a second glance in a garden setting if attractively presented. A washing-line of the rotary sort in a tidy backyard is not a cynosure, but a clothes-line of clean laundry billowing between two apple trees is a happy sight. The garden props that cost nothing can be everyday objects left in a place where they will be noticed. The abandoned wheelbarrow, garden roller or watering-can, even the fork in the vegetable patch, give a feeling of human scale to the landscape. They suggest that the person who was using them has disappeared for a moment, but will shortly be back to start work again. Cloches or forcing pots in the beds are reassuring reminders of order and love of plants. The ideas that we attach to visual objects are often more important than the things themselves. In the eighteenth century, urns were used in the landscape to prompt thoughts of mortality; such morbidity is less fashionable today, but the principle of suggesting tricks of association can still be a valuable one – especially if the object has had, or continues to have, a useful working life.

Just as tools and garden artefacts suggest honest toil and love of gardening, so stones and shells can be made to evoke friends and far-off places. Gardens are good backgrounds for the virtually free props that don't have an appropriate place indoors. The irresistible stone found on the beach can be brought home and arranged with other holiday reminders on a wall or a flat stone table. The shells that occupied an afternoon of searching on a distant shore will continue to be

OPPOSITE ABOVE Forcing pots are always an adornment in the kitchen garden. On the far right, traditional pots for rhubarb are still in place among the leaves. These are expensive to buy, but old chimney pots can be a cheaper alternative. Near right, six seakale pots make a pyramid at the end of a path; just visible in the foreground are the grey leaves of the seakale that was forced under them earlier in the year.

engaging near a pool or a fountain, where they can be kept wet. The animal bones, fir-cones, fossils and lumps of wood which are the inspiration of many modern sculptors can be a private source of wonder. And if this sounds pretentious, if natural wonders can never for you be art, think instead of these objects' associations and use them as reminders of the places where they were found, or of the people who brought them to the garden.

Where the objects are treated as collections, a corner of the garden becomes a private natural history museum. Groups of curiosities –

ABOVE Protecting crops from the depredations of birds is often necessary. These pots on sticks with a net thrown over them look friendlier than a high-tech rectangle of steel tubes and netting, and probably cost rather less to install.
OPPOSITE BELOW The Victorian iron-framed handlight has a much longer life than its plastic counterpart and is unlikely to be blown away. For precious seedlings, or an early flower which might be spoiled by bad weather, handlights like this can be useful as well as beautiful.

the stones that look like faces, the driftwood that resembles a monster -- can provide interest and a focus for a corner that lacks a view. Nature's cast-offs can also be arranged in patterns, as they formerly were in grottoes, or in the houses of those late-eighteenth-century spinsters who spent their days setting out ferns, feathers or molluscs in decorative ways. Found things, as our ancestors knew, are not difficult to display. It is, after all, not unlike the grouping of flowers to create pictures. With inanimate objects the task is easier, because you are only dealing with shapes and not with a change in scale and colour.

ABOVE AND OPPOSITE ABOVE
Utilitarian objects like pumps, buckets, brushes and baths have become collectors' items. Where they can be incorporated into the working garden, they cease to look like museum pieces; water pumps can even be used, provided an electric attachment is fitted to preclude any great effort. Galvanized watering-cans are also popular. They are heavier to use than plastic ones, but look less alien in a garden. Left on a path, a bright green watering-can will blow over in the first puff of wind, but these stay where you put them until they are needed again.

OPPOSITE BELOW Baskets fit in well out of doors, because they are made of natural materials. For dead-heading and hand-weeding it is essential to have something light and portable that can be carried around as the work is done. Keeping a wheelbarrow in line with operations can interrupt the pace of dead-heading. It is easier to use a wicker basket like the one under the rose-bush and tip it into the barrow when it is full. It is, besides, a better shape for serious gardening than a wooden trug because there is no danger of petals or the light seeds of weeds being blown back on to the bed. For gardeners who can never find the secateurs or the trowel that they have just put down, the wicker tool-carrier might be just the thing.

Scarecrows

Scarecrows are an excuse for a touch of fantasy. Not only a device for frightening the birds away from growing plants, these traditionally ragged figures can also take a positively attractive form. The woman with the artificial butterfly perched on her planter's straw hat (right) is intended to entice rather than to repel – though whether real butterflies might be encouraged by this method it is hard to say. The 'brush' man with a bird-box head (opposite, below right) is also designed to welcome small birds rather than scare them, even if he does look a little grim. All scarecrows have something in common with snowmen: they are ephemeral creatures and their clothes will not stand up to years of exposure. Left outside for too long, they become unrecognizable and, as they deteriorate, those

that are meant to scare the birds become too familiar to be effective. Contraptions that flap or rustle will work better over time than figures that stand stock still. In country districts scarecrows are still popular, however, with an added refinement: a transistor radio in the pocket of the scarecrow's coat keeps the sound of voices always in the air.

Sensitive gardeners, who prefer not to contemplate a home-made model of a vagrant, can buy dummy versions of birds of prey to hang over the crops (right), or tin cats with glassy eyes to stand among the Brussels sprouts (left). No scarecrow is ever one hundred per cent effective, but most of them cost very little to make and will at least provide something to talk about. The frustrated artist can find an outlet for his creativity that is fun as well as useful.

TOP Old hand-thrown pots like these, which vary in colour and texture, are very desirable; smooth machine-made pots lack character. In a greenhouse plastic pots are useful, but for standing plants out–side in summer terracotta looks better and is more substantial.

ABOVE AND OPPOSITE A beautifully made compost heap, surrounded by straw bales that have gradually subsided into the heap, waits to be spread around the flowers and vegetables. The orderly potting shed, with its row of cleaned spades, catches a shaft of sunlight when the

door is left ajar. In large gardens that are open to the public, a glimpse of the potting shed is always a bonus. Even where the house and garden is only a tenth of the size of these showplaces, a tidy array of tools can be a pleasure to contemplate and is within everyone's means.

BELOW It is a joy to see a well–tended and orderly garden. Here the standard roses have been prepared for a hard winter. Wrapped in hessian, they should come through wind and frost unscathed to welcome another spring. Modern materials might do the job as well, but plastic sheeting would never present such an agreeable sight. Where tender wall plants need covering, dried bracken or branches of fir can be used; several layers should be enough to protect the roots from winter damage, but if the body of the plant is threatened this needs further precautions. Home-made insulation for out of doors can be contrived from two large pieces of chicken wire nailed to posts the height of the plant. Between the inner and outer ring, bracken, dried leaves or straw can be trapped all the way up so that the plant has its own winter duvet.

BOTTOM The bunches of onions hanging in the sun to dry them out for winter provide another example of the beauty of a job properly done. In France the harvested crops of onion and garlic are traditionally attached to a woven rush plait.

LEFT AND BELOW Making a virtue of a necessity is a good precept for gardeners on a shoestring. In large gardens woodsheds can occupy forgotten and unvisited corners, but in small country gardens they can be an adornment to the landscape. The art of arranging layers of logs, such as under this lean-to roof, presents a satisfying effect as well as being the most economical use of space. Such orderliness raised to an art form has been perfected in cold northern countries, where wood is often vital to winter comfort.

Gardeners who like to be in control of their environment would do well to emulate the examples of good housekeeping shown here. Even where there is no cover for storing wood, logs can be stacked into tidy heaps, as these have been, for the sap to dry out. The sight of so much dry wood immediately suggests the comforting warmth of winter fires indoors.

Rocks and Stones

In large gardens, cool lawns provide a rest from the brightness of flowers. The silent spaces are harder to arrange on a smaller scale, but the restraint that every garden needs can come from stones and greenery. Rocks are a feature of Japanese Zen gardens, where flat stones are placed to encourage contemplation. Rolling stones, as everyone knows, gather no moss; by implication a moss-covered stone has been where it lies for a long time. The flat, mossy stones under the tree (opposite above) look peaceful, settled and calming.

The boulders bordering the path (opposite below) have a different message. They might appeal to lovers of the curious or fantastic, for large lumps of rock are in the best picturesque tradition. At the end of the eighteenth century in England, rugged rocks, stagheaded trees, and beggars' hovels in the distance were admired because they provided the drama and decay which seemed so lacking in the polite parks of the time. A similarly disturbing spectacle is provided in modern gardens by the odd out-of-scale feature, but it has to be big enough to provoke a reaction of awe. The large rock on the right would need several men to move it and even the smaller ones on the left of the path could not be shifted by one person alone. Having immovable natural objects in the garden is a humbling reminder of man's feebleness in the face of nature. Large stones like these act as a warning of elemental powers; they are not for those who want their gardens to be safe domestic havens.

A small stone surrounded by primroses (far left) is more curious than awesome, but such rocks were, too, favourites with eighteenth-century gardeners. Grotto stones, all bumps and holes like this river-riddled piece of limestone, were piled into heaps or built into caverns in the sides of hills to make damp retreats for summer days. Looked at individually, these stones are intriguing. Some have so many holes that they resemble skulls; others look like miniature landscape features. Sometimes, a single stone can be more arresting than a whole rockery. All large stones, even the ones carved by man, like the millstone now lapped in ferns (centre), have the power to stop people in their tracks.

Tall plants make gardens mysterious. Where walls for climbers are in short supply, or space for trees or shrubs limited, maintain the vertical interest by using props for plants.

Plant Supports

LEFT AND ABOVE In a painting artists often use the geometry of a triangle to pull a composition together. The same shape can also help to structure a garden. Once the netting around these smooth canes has been covered by scrambling plants, the shape will lose its distinction but will still be recognizable. The painted blue pyramid for roses has a more assertive presence.

Vertical gardening adds an extra territory for gardeners who are pinched for space. In minimal plots there may not be room for a tree, but high-rise climbers on a variety of supports can make the garden seem at once more exciting as well as more abundant. Imagine a small town garden planted with low bright flowers, and then think of the same area broken up by a few tall posts, with climbing plants attached – even this, most basic of garden spaces, instantly responds to a change of level. In winter, summer-performing climbers will be bony and bare, but the supports themselves will continue to provide something to look at, so it might as well be something agreeable.

Iron arches, a feature of late Victorian gardens, have had an immense revival recently, so that sometimes they may seem overdone. Where arches always work is when they are used along a path that ends in a framed view or feature; they lose their point when the pathway leads nowhere. In winter, unless it is supporting evergreens or strong plants like apples, a metal arch can look chilly and unprepossessing clad only in the remnants of a rose and a wisp of brown clematis. If you see them from your windows, wooden pergolas made out of sturdy trellis-work or rustic posts look friendlier while the climbers have gone into hibernation. Wood is always an inoffensive material out of doors; it may not last as long as metal, but by the time the pergola or trellis has to be renewed, it may be time for a change anyway.

A run of arches or a pergola occupies a fair amount of space and in most gardens simpler structures will prove less demanding. Formal gardeners will approve of wooden pyramids or obelisks for training roses, which make an important shape in any flower bed. Cheaper and easier to make – and just as helpful to roses – are wigwams of strong poles lashed together at the top with string. On both these arrangements roses can have their branches pinned in downward curving arcs, so that flower buds break all along the shoot and cover the structure with a summer's growth. The difference between the two constructions is that the pyramid obelisk is meant to be seen, whereas the wigwam is unpretentious and practical; it all depends on your style.

The framework for any trained plant that loses its leaves in winter needs some thought, for six months is a long time to live with an ugly support system. Pleached and espaliered trees may be better on good round posts with wires unobtrusively placed, than on rusty angle iron with bright green plastic-coated wires, unless of course the latter was what you happened to want.

In the vegetable plot, too, there is scope for tailoring the practical to your own vision. Peas and beans can be grown in a variety of ways,

and it makes sense to choose one that you enjoy looking at. Rows of smooth canes and string suit some people, others will prefer a line of old-fashioned peasticks cut from hazels. Nor are rows the only way of growing climbing crops. They can be set in a maypole arrangement around one post with a skirt of strings, or grown up a wigwam of poles. They can be made to run over arches, or they can be trained to trelliswork. Choosing how to grow the plants is almost as much fun as choosing what to grow.

FAR LEFT AND LEFT Gertrude Jekyll, the famous Edwardian garden designer, favoured stout structures for pergolas and free-standing supports. Her advice is still sound: there is something unnerving about a structure that looks in danger of imminent collapse from the weight of its climbers. Both the rustic arch (far left), and the handsome trellis of larch poles behind it (seen in close-up, left) look reassuringly solid, and both have supporting diagonals for extra strength.

Roses often prefer the airy arrangement of a pergola or free-standing structure to being grown on a wall, where varieties that are susceptible to mildew are more likely to succumb. Habit is important: roses for pergolas should be chosen for flowers that hang down. Varieties like 'New Dawn' would carry all their blooms in the air above the roof, but old-fashioned cluster varieties will dangle down before your eyes.

BELOW Wisteria is always a good candidate for a pergola, because its flowers hang below its branches, Laburnum and vines are equally obliging, and all of these will twine and trail along the supports provided for them. These plants were Regency favourites for their drooping habit, although they were more often grown on iron supports than on wood.

ABOVE AND OPPOSITE Temporary structures for annuals offer the chance to exercise some ingenuity. The pyramid of bean poles tied with string (top) is a more rustic version of the bamboos and netting seen on page 96. But the sweet peas that have started to grow will need help if they are to climb the string ladder, as they are inclined to go into reverse and climb down themselves if their tendrils are faced with an expanse of air. The crossing diagonals of bamboos (above), where the peas are being grown, would also need some supervision in the early stages. The twiggier peasticks (opposite), with their crowns of woven hazel, offer a more encouraging ascent for plants because there are plenty of places for tendrils to cling to on the way up. Light sticks, like all the ones shown here, need to be driven as far into the ground as they will go, because they will have to support the weight of plants, and possibly stand up to strong winds later in the year.

RIGHT A small aluminium support like this might be a better host for a stronger plant than sweet peas, which will tend to fall out from its empty spaces. A vine, for example, might be carefully trained to each of the four corners and allowed to cross the horizontal bars, so that it follows the shape of the metalwork. The hanging bunches of grapes would be easy to admire and pick and the shape of the frame would not be lost, as it soon might be here with the sweet peas.

BELOW Steel corkscrews, such as these, make very effective supports for those varieties of tomato that like to twine. Tomato plants are often grown up strings. This can cause problems, however, as the weight of the fruit sometimes makes the tomato vine too heavy for thin string, and there is a risk that it may cut into the plant.

ABOVE Small trees around the lily pond are here being trained to fill triangular templates of bamboo. This is a similar system to pleaching, but instead of the trees being extended in one flat plane to meet each other, they remain free-standing, their branches trained out to right and left from the trunk. Such uncompromising shapes suggest a rigid formality, which may need to be maintained elsewhere in the garden. The scrambling roses at one tree's foot look charming while both are young, but may eventually be at odds. Anarchy in the garden can intrigue, but the effect can also be uncomfortable when tousled elements present not so much a contrast to an overall message of formality, as a threat.

At the edge of a country garden, this row of traditional bean-poles cut from hazels looks almost too beautiful to cover. Until manual labour became prohibitively expensive, the coppicing of native woodland was widely practised in Europe. Trees like ash, hazel and birch were grown as multi-stemmed shrubs and then had their branches cut out at ground level as they became mature enough to use. Some were destined for firewood, some for the handles of tools and others, like these, to support vegetable crops. Coppicing is good conservation practice and in the green 1990s it has become possible to find sources of cut bean-poles again. Where woodland is being managed traditionally it is worth asking if bean-poles and pea-sticks are available. They rarely find their way into garden centres, but they do exist in areas where coppicing is practised.

Gardeners with space for a few rows of hazel bushes might grow their own poles and pea-sticks. Hazels grow fast and a seven- to ten-year cycle should provide branches of a respectable length for cutting. As well as bean-poles, hazels can also be used to make hoops for training old-fashioned roses. For this, a long hazel branch is bent over as far as it will go and both ends of the branch are pushed into the ground. Three of these arcs should be enough to encircle a rose bush. The shoots of the rose are then pulled down and tied on to the curves of hazel, so that the rose branches also make a series of arches. In winter the whole thing looks like a crab. All roses flower better if their shoots can be trained downwards, because flower buds will break along the whole length of a curved branch rather than just at the tip, as they do if they grow vertically.

Enclosures

Many plants can be trained to create an outdoor room or passage. Squares of pleached trees, like limes in a corner of a shady garden, (below left) make roofless rooms where a square of sky forms the ceiling. In hot places the sky can be shut out by trees or climbers, like vines and wisteria, trained along wires high above human heads (below right). But green caves, with a place to sit and watch sunshine through a filter of leaves, are only tempting in brilliant summers. On a wet, grey day the effect would be the ultimate in dankness so this is not something to try in the unreliable north, unless there is space to spare.

Fruit tunnels (right) provide perhaps the most satisfactory of all green ceilings. A corridor of apples or pears can be cheerful even on a rainy day and fruit blossom is one of the best sights of spring in any garden. Fruit arches can be spaced – as they are here – so that a rhythm of light and dark is created as you walk under the tunnel, or they can be trained to form a canopy. They were a feature in early European gardens, where shady walks were preferred to sunny paths; today, with the arrival of mass-produced ironwork, tunnels have become deservedly popular again. Each apple or pear tree is trained and pruned like an individual cordon; netting can be flung over the arch in summer to protect the fruit from birds.

What's afoot in a garden – the mood and style of a place – is defined
by what is underfoot. It is a sad fact that most of us cannot walk
along a path or up and down stairs without looking at the ground.

Groundworks

LEFT This lemon-tiled staircase rises gently past the trunk of a tree: an arrangement that needs no flowers. Mediterranean in spirit, tiles like these might warm up a town basement area in the cold north.
ABOVE The green 'pointing' to these bricks is a happy touch. Since the plants will ultimately creep over the paving, it is best used in areas that don't get heavy wear.

What's afoot in a garden – the mood and style of a place – is defined by what is underfoot. It is a sad fact that most of us cannot walk along a path or up and down stairs without looking at the ground. If you have to pick your way through mud, or take care not to stumble on the stones, you may never enjoy the flowers. Reassuring and unobtrusive natural surfaces that blend well with existing surroundings are usually the best choice, when the plants are what matter most. Put groundworks of modern materials in a cottage setting and, however hard the roses riot or the honeysuckle tumbles, the tinted concrete paviors will grab all the attention. But just as a beautiful dress can be diminished by an ill-chosen pair of shoes, so in a garden the flower beds need to be set off by the right footwear.

All groundworks are keepers of the balance between peace and motion in a garden. They can restore order and calm when a scene is too busy, or the man-made elements can be used to bring life and interest to dull places. A path may seem an insignificant part of the garden picture, but the total area of hard surface underfoot is made to seem larger because it consists of one continuous material. This is rare in the muddled plant havens of today's plots. Think of a road carving through green fields; the effect it has on the landscape is a magnified version of the garden path. The continuous ribbon of grey may seem dull compared with the green of grass and trees, but it is the image of the road that remains, confronting the eye with a distant band of hard surface. Paths, unlike roads, can vary in their static qualities. Concrete, which has no variation in texture or colour, will always appear as dead space. Sometimes this may be what you want. If the planting scheme is jazzy and leaps from spike to spike in bright jagged patches, a dead surface between flower beds may be just what is required. Where leaves are bold and smooth, some texture in a

path may be better than a plain material. A bed of irises, for example, with their grey sword-shaped leaves, would not be improved by a dull grey path, but might look very satisfying next to a run of bricks.

Sometimes the groundworks -- the hard landscaping – can stand in for the plants. An extreme example of this is seen on page 108. With a staircase of lemons, who needs flowers? Similarly, mosaics and complicated pebble patterns are better left in an uncluttered space; they provide all the ornament that is needed. Adding decoration in the form of flowers would make for an overdose of colour and pattern.

Steps are, in any case, demanding features that you cannot fail to notice, even without lemons, so they need to fit in with the overall mood. In very grand gardens, flights of more than five risers will not look out of place, but in smaller settings it is often better to turn the steps sideways on to a wall than to be confronted by a large number of centrally placed ones. All steps need to be comfortable, with treads that are never less than 30 cm (1 ft) wide and risers that are no more than 20 cm (8 in) high. Even these measurements do not allow for a very relaxed progress and stairs are better made wider and shallower than this basic pattern if at all possible.

TOP Old or second-hand bricks give colour and texture to the garden. RIGHT AND RIGHT ABOVE Brick can look daunting over large areas, but in paths the pavers can point the way. Herringbone formation suggests arrows; stretcher bond has the bricks laid end to end.

FAR RIGHT Mixing stone slabs amidst the brick is another way of avoiding too much brick in larger areas. It is important to choose hard-wearing bricks, as those used for walls will crumble in time; a little decay adds patina to a garden, but total disintegration is to be avoided.

RIGHT A mixture of knapped flints
and rough-hewn stone runs a tex-
tured curve through a tidy garden.
With all paths of uneven materials
drainage can be a problem, as water
will lodge in the cracks if a good
run-off is not arranged. Where a
path slopes, this is easy to manage,
but on the flat it will have to be
done by raising the central section,
as here, so that the water runs down
to the sides. Laying a similar path to
this one would not be something
for the inexperienced to tackle.
FAR RIGHT Green paths through
long grass with wild flowers have
become a late twentieth-century
favourite. As well as being ecologi-
cally sound, they are labour-saving.
More bees and butterflies are the
result of less mowing, but the long
grass does need to be cut after the
wild flowers have seeded and again
before the summer ends. Even with
a strimmer this is hard work,
because the grass must be carried
away to be composted or burnt.
Grass paths are not hard-wearing
and if the winter route for heavy
barrows lies through an orchard,
like in the photograph above, by
the spring the path will be mud
rather than grass. The narrow row
of bricks here prevents this damage
by giving the barrow a hard-tracked
route to follow.

TOP LEFT A wooden decking path is only a possibility where timber is freely available; perhaps the most appropriate place in a garden for timber on the ground is near water, where it feels like being on a boat.

TOP RIGHT Gravel was popular with the Victorians for paths; many plants love to grow into it.
ABOVE This band of bricks is an effective edging to serviceable bark chippings.

OPPOSITE Large shingle, such as this, is generally easier to maintain than pea-sized stones, because it stays where it is put and should not end up on the lawn, the gardener's boots or the flower bed.

Patterns with Pebbles

Hard surfaces in gardens tend to be expensive because of the labour involved in laying them. For those who can do things for themselves, using good materials, everything is affordable. Laying pebbles in patterns is not as difficult as it looks. Draw your pattern on to graph paper first. Level the surface, and stretch over it a string grid, the strings spaced 25 cm or one foot apart. The pebbles are set

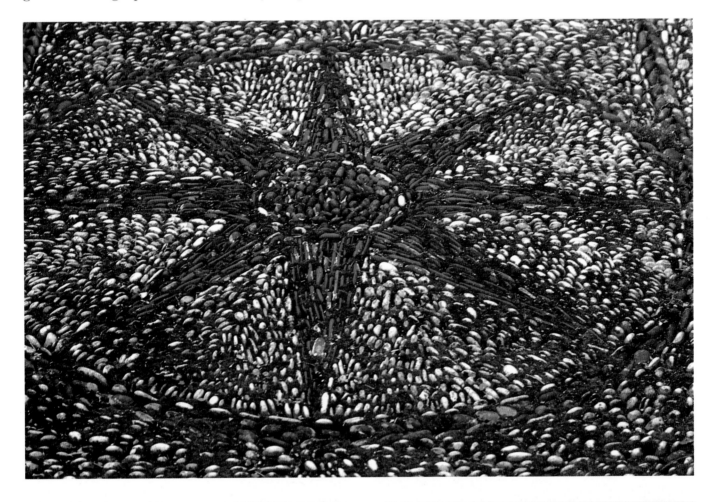

in a dry mix of sand and a very little cement. Ideally they should touch each other, or the pattern will end up with more infill than pebble. But if the mosaic ends up with a few stones out of line, it will not matter too much. Like a Persian carpet where a deliberate mistake is included to show that the rug is handmade, your mosaic will proclaim its originality.

ABOVE AND RIGHT In informal or wild places steps are difficult to arrange, because they can so often look too imposing for their setting. A straight flight of half a dozen stairs may not sound grand, but because of the amount of space needed, it may end up looking out of scale with the rest of the garden. Ideally, the risers should be 20 cm (8 in) high and the treads could be double that. Although there is some scope for making steps steeper or shallower, the treads cannot comfortably be narrower than about 30 cm (1 ft). In these pictures, the problems of getting from one level to another have been solved without spoiling the mood of the planting. At the top of the woodland garden (above), shallow timber risers retain broad gravel steps that lead down to a dropping curve of path, set with stepping stones. There is a danger that these stones may become too slippery to walk on in winter, but the path has a friendly and unpretentious look; equally suitable are the stone slab steps in another informal garden (top). The narrow stone steps (right) allow enough room for one person to walk; covered in plants as they are, they could never look imposing.

BELOW The cut-stone treads of these more formal steps are so densely planted that the galaxy of daisies has all but covered them. Cut stone is beyond the dreams of budget gardeners, but with this treatment even concrete, with a layer of ground stone dust on top, might be acceptable.

BOTTOM The semi-circle of brick steps are also covered with plants. Wild strawberries and moss have colonized the bricks, which can be a help when the brickwork is of a less than professional standard. Plants will cover a lot of deficiencies in the building, as well as adding an instant aged look to new groundworks. Where steps are combined with a wall, as they have been here, a semi-circular flight is a neat arrangement. If they had been built straight, the steps would have had to be retained by a raised edge on either side, or they could have been set back into the wall, but either way they would occupy much more space. Another trick for minimizing the space taken up by steps is to set them so that you walk up the flight parallel to the wall – as on old barns. This may be a good plan where more than half a dozen steps are needed.

*A shady place to rest from the sun, or somewhere to take shelter when
it rains, all gardens need signs of human habitation if they are not
to appear as wildernesses.*

Rooms Outside

In down-to-earth gardens, showy buildings often seem out of place.
The gloss of conservatories belongs more perhaps to the world of the
interior rather than to gardens. Ready-made arbours and pavilions
tend to be expensive: they suggest money and inorganic origins that can strike an unsympathetic note in natural surroundings. Yet buildings and shelters do have a place out of
doors, because they are humanizing. It is the balance of
power between man and nature that gives a garden the necessary drama to bring it to life. However green it may sound,
a tangled wilderness in Sleeping-Beauty-style does not count
as a garden, because gardens are made for people to make
use of – if they are to be really enjoyable places, they need to
have a place to keep the tools, a shelter from extreme weather, or just somewhere to sit and watch the birds; all of these will add
to the pleasure of being out of doors.

LEFT Trellis partitions need not
cost a fortune. This ogee-arched
arbour was quickly made from the
cheapest expandable garden centre
panels, under a top cut out of marine
ply. The blue-green colour, here
stained rather than painted, is a good
foil for plants.
ABOVE Stained timber behind a
crimson clematis; this green is also a
good colour for out of doors.

Even in the grandest places, garden buildings are traditionally
less polished versions of the houses they adorn, and modest houses
need simple structures if they are not to look ridiculous. A classical
temple in the grounds of a bungalow could be called 'Folly de
Grandeur', but the joke might pall after a bit and, as jokes go, built
ones come rather expensive.

Sometimes existing buildings can be adapted and adorned to give
them a new life. A disused coal shed or an outdoor privy can be
cleared and cleaned; with the doors removed and a few climbers
growing over the roof even the most utilitarian of buildings can be
transformed into a cool place to sit and watch the birds. Where there
is no existing outbuilding to be adapted, a simple arrangement of
wooden posts and trellis is neither difficult nor expensive to arrange.
In natural wood, round posts tend to look better than square ones
(unless the square ones are of hardwood and at least 10 cm/4 inches

thick, which puts them out of most people's price range). Larch poles can be bought with bark attached, but they will not last as long as those which have been pressure-treated, and if they are to be sunk in the ground this is important. A stained rather than a painted finish might suit your style better, especially if you want the structure to merge into the background. Alternatively, you can make paint look old and weather-beaten by using emulsion or undercoat rather than a glossy oil. It will not last as long, but on a small scale it will not take too much time to redo.

Garden buildings to accommodate human beings may be over-large for gardeners who are pinched for space, but even the tiniest plot may have enough room to incorporate a beehive, a dovecote or a bird table, which will suggest that here nature and man are working in harmony. Gardens where there is no movement of birds and butter-flies are sterile, unnatural places. Chickens, doves and bees are a delight to see but they can be demanding for their keeper. Wild birds, however, are almost self-sufficient, although they will appreciate a bird bath in summer. In the hungry winter months, when they threaten fruit buds and seedlings, a bird table will keep them from foraging among the gardener's plants and give enormous pleasure to the watch-er from the window.

BELOW AND RIGHT Trellised shelters provide a welcome refuge from the sun. The seating can be as simple as the bare bench in the porch (below left), or a chair behind the metal table (opposite), which can be cleared of its pots of flowers for meals. For an all-year round arrangement a roof of glass is the answer. The fretwork gothic frieze (below right) edges on to a lean-to glass roof. The frieze's design was based on a nineteenth-century model seen in a railway station. Machine-cut from marine plywood, it has a useful as well as a decorative function in that it hides the gutter catching the water from the sloping glass roof. Against a wall absorbing the rays of the late-after-noon sun, the shelter keeps tender plants dry throughout the winter. Such an arrangement provides the illusion of a conservatory for those on a modest budget, and allows meals to be taken out of doors very early in the year, when the sun shines through the panes of glass on to the table below. Later on, when the vine is in leaf, the conservatory will become a leafy bower decorated with plenty of geraniums and fuch-sias in pots.

Trellis for shelters outside can be either wooden or metalwork, but metal will probably last longer, as rust is slower to set in than the rot that will ultimately prove the down-fall of softwood. Maintenance is important for both sorts and they will need to be kept painted or treated, as rainwater tends to collect in the angles of the trellis. Lattice trellis is probably easier to manage when it is square- rather than dia-mond-shaped, but it never looks quite as pretty.

ABOVE In this summer-house a pot of succulents sits on the windowsill ready to be enjoyed at eye-level. Their glamorous leaves are a good match for the ice-blue paintwork on the wooden boards below.

RIGHT Garden sheds are often hidden from view, but in a corner of a painter's allotment, this simple wooden building adds definition and human scale to an abundant array of plants. Without the shed, the brightly coloured flowers might seem gaudy and pointless; with it they look domestic and cheerful. The clay pantiles give the building some distinction and make it seem solid enough to inhabit – an agreeable place to spend a wet afternoon, sketching the flowers outside the window, tidying tools, or sorting pots. In small spaces garden storage can be difficult to incorporate. Here it has been made a feature and the detail of the painted roof board shows trouble taken.

Animal houses

Chickens, it cannot be denied, are a bit of a liability in the garden. Their fondness for taking dust baths among favourite plants can be provocative for the gardener. They also need to be kept out of jaws of foxes, but if you can accept their limitations and have room for a chicken house (below and opposite below), they are a very desirable feature, especially the rarer breeds. If hens sound like too much work, an aviary cage (with slightly smaller holes in the netting) can be a place for small ornamental birds which will not put the garden at risk. Bees too are an adornment if you are brave enough to keep them (right), but for the settled sight of doves on

your own dovecote you do not need to make such an effort (opposite, top). Many people who are prepared to take the trouble to keep indoor pets consider outdoor ones too difficult, but birds do not have to be taken for walks, nor will they sit on the sofa or bite the baby. A cockerel may wake the neighbours, it is true, but birds have more to offer the gardener than dogs or cats, which can be very unhelpful in the flower beds.

LEFT A yellow door fits neatly between stone walls. Close-boarding is traditional for back doors and outhouses; such a design, one that has been in use for years, gives a garden a settled feeling. Against brick the colour would have been less pleasing but here, reinforcing the gold tints in the stone and the colour of the well-placed lilies, it is delightful.

TOP Here a corrugated tin hut has been cleverly hung with straw matting, which has been tacked to wooden battens, so that from afar the building looks as if it disappears into the background. If you want to make a feature of a shed, however, there is nothing wrong with corrugated iron, particularly if painted rust red or dark green.

ABOVE LEFT AND RIGHT Against a wall, a tiny lean-to greenhouse provides storage space for tender plants and seedlings. Lean-to houses are cheaper to heat than free-standing ones and when painted black you would have to look hard to find it. Also making use of a wall, a shelter for wood with a cross frame is an agreeable sight.

'Green' Rooms

Most 'green' rooms, where the plants provide the walls, need a little help from man. The solid wall of yew (right) embracing a table and chairs proves the exception; the semi-circle of hedge will shelter those inside from wind, and on warm days will probably be a suntrap. The larch poles that underpin the other 'green' rooms here are the garden architect's cheapest and best ally. Repton, the eighteenth and early nineteenth-century landscape designer, created arbours with substantial arches boasting triangular pediments and finials of fir-cones. Edwin Lutyens and Gertrude Jekyll, design partners in

*the Edwardian age, also used wood for pergolas and arbours, often
combined with stone piers. Larch poles are particularly adaptable.
At their simplest they can be placed across the corner where two walls
meet, to create a support for a vine (left, top). A closer screen,
infilled with sloping diagonals made of thinner poles than the main
supports, can also be very attractive (left and far left). It is better to
keep the carpentry simple: conventional rustic work, with lots of
short crosspieces from corner to corner, can look restless if not well
done. Softwood frameworks are not long-lived unless pressure-
treated; but some wood preservers can poison plants.*

The pleasure of seeing cool ponds or places for birds to splash and
toads to hide is an enduring one. Modern gardeners treat water as
an even more precious commodity than our ancestors did.

Watery Effects

Deep in our collective subconscious lies the knowledge that where water is, there peace and plenty will be found. Early man made the first priority of any early settlement finding a source of water that

could be used to keep men, beasts and crops alive. The earliest gardeners made water a central feature of their designs, and its precious value to the modern grower has in no way diminished with its arrival by means of the reservoir and pipe. We still treat water with a reverence and delight that must be built into the human psyche from centuries of

LEFT A round stone basin at the heart of a woodland planting provides a resting-place for the eye and a relief from the formless mass of plants. Without the water the plants would be duller; with it, they appear almost magical.
ABOVE A carved dipping-well provides a cool spot to sit and trail your fingers on a hot day.

dependence. Ancient Persians and Indians, as well as Renaissance Italians, admired the sound of 'a thousand fountains, a thousand rivulets, a thousand rills' – those splashes and trickles cannot have sounded so very different from what we might hear today on a summer's day. There is nothing like water in a garden for making time stand still.

Fountains and waterfalls have never been easier to arrange. With modern submersible pumps, ideal for small pools, even small-scale gardeners can run to a fountain a metre (3ft) high. Provided the water is clear – and if it is kept on the move it will be – it does not matter how small the effect in a garden. In the classical tradition, a simple lead pipe sticking out from a wall, dripping water into a stone basin that is then pumped round in a perpetual cycle, will give you the sound of running water. To make this more sophisticated you can put the pipe through a fountain mask, or a few well-chosen rocks, or have an upper basin overflowing into a lower one.

Ponds and pools that are meant to look natural are easy to install and not expensive. The easiest to handle are fibreglass or solid liners, but they can be hard to camouflage. Linings made from flexible butyl rubber or plastic sheeting, which can be weighted with large stones at the edges and planted with water-loving plants around the sides, are often more convincing. Both liners create the sort of watery places to attract wildlife, but the water can become scummy if it is not kept oxygenated either with a pump or underwater plants. Pools intended for plants need to be sighted in a sunny place and away from large trees, as decaying leaves always cause problems in water. Whatever the size or purpose of a pool, it is worth remembering that water is as fascinating to small children as it is to grown-ups. Anyone creating a pool in the garden should bear in mind that water to the depth of as little as 45 cm (18 in) is enough to drown a small child.

Summer droughts and a general anxiety about the depletion of nature's resources have elevated water to near-sacred status in the garden. Without it, we know all too well, our gardens would cease to exist, and without ponds and pools there would be no places for birds to splash and toads to hide. So rainwater off roofs can be collected into butts and barrels, to be used to water vegetables or plants. Plunging a can into a container of water is quicker than filling it from a tap, and in times of extreme drought the same containers can be sited under the bathroom window to be filled with water siphoned from the bath.

RIGHT, ABOVE Rafts of wooden decking make giant stepping-bridges over this pond in a Dutch designer's garden.
FAR RIGHT, ABOVE A fountain is all the more spectacular if it falls on shells of mother-of-pearl, because it keeps the pearl in a state of perpetual iridescence. Here the spray captures a shaft of light and transfers it to everything it touches.
RIGHT AND FAR RIGHT Small stone vessels, full of water catching reflections of the leaves above, might serve as bird-baths or as reservoirs of water in a wild corner. The large-leaved plants near the round troughs heighten the atmosphere.

ABOVE LEFT Beachcombing for beautiful stones and shells is a compulsive pleasure, but pebbles so lovingly collected on seaside holidays tend to look disappointing when you bring them home because as they dry out they fade. Here they are revived in a glistening array by the steady trickle from a wall-mounted fountain. This original design, made for a town garden, is echoed in the shapes of the box balls in pots, which look like green additions to the pebble collection.

ABOVE RIGHT Wall fountains are less showy than free-standing fountains, but they are the ones to choose for quiet places and more modest settings. If all you want to hear is the gentle chuckle of water, such an arrangement can be installed by an amateur in an afternoon. Here a rather more elaborate example of a wall fountain shows a curtain of ivy which falls around the stone trough. Water, stone and greenery make beautiful companions; flowers are unnecessary.

RIGHT Bamboo pipes arranged in Japanese style create watery music. As the water falls through the hollow stems, it makes an eerie noise like a wind instrument played underwater. Varying notes can also be heard if water falls from different heights on to flat stones. Sir Geoffrey Jellicoe, one of this century's greatest garden designers, contrived to make water play treble, alto, tenor and bass chords by causing it to fall over pieces of V-shaped copper at Shute House in Dorset.

BELOW AND BOTTOM There is
something so calm, complete and
satisfying about a circle of water that
contrivance is unnecessary in what
surrounds it. The bowl mounted on
a platform of stones makes a digni-
fied focus among cow parsley and
ferns, while the dipping-well (below)
retains its original pump.

LEFT Galvanized watering cans are heavier to use than plastic ones, but there is no denying their charm. This is the sort of can that Beatrix Potter painted for Peter Rabbit to hide in, the kind that you expect to find in gardens run on the best traditional lines. Left on the path for the water to warm up in the sun, it can be used to water nearby pots and flower beds. Watering of seedlings should always be done with a rose on the end of the can, and if this is turned upside-down, so that the holes in the rose face the sky, the spray will be even gentler.

ABOVE A stream, with water cascading over natural boulders, is every gardener's dream. This is the place for plants that love to be at the water's edge, like these candelabra primulas. Bog plants never look right in flower beds, where they tend to wilt because they need damp air and cool soil at their roots. The temptation to indulge in a variety of plants that enjoy wet places is strong if you are lucky enough to live near water. This planting, where the primulas have been allowed to colonize the banks of a stream just as they do when at home in Tibet, illustrates the advantages of restraint.

Fences and hedges give a garden an instant setting. Their enclosure provides a personal space, with privacy and shelter, where plants can be seen against the backdrop that suits them best.

Boundaries and Dividers

Boundaries and fences are the frame to the garden picture. Just as a painting can be transformed by its frame, so too can a garden be improved by a surround that focuses the eye. One of the principal aims of the garden designer is to impose a human scale and a private atmosphere on a place. At its most extreme, this might be illustrated by the example of a house and garden on the side of a wild hill. Without any enclosure, however beautiful the flowers, they would never compete with the view, which would probably cause a mild attack of agoraphobia. A panorama is lovely to look at, but wide open spaces are not for being in every day of your life, and an unrestricted one-hundred-and-eighty-degree foreground view can often seem bleak and daunting.

LEFT Imagine the crown imperials seen against a background of green without the wooden fence that shows them off so well; they would be less dramatic without it, and less so, too, without the box edging at their feet. Here the fence and hedge emphasize vertical and horizontal lines around the flowers.
ABOVE Against a fence of strong trellis, poppies stand out clearly.

In the absence of a view, boundaries become important for what they conceal. The cars, the neighbours and the ugly skyline can all, with a bit of strategic planning, be banished from your garden. For shelter from the unseen – the noise or wind that can break the spell you are trying to create – barriers are also important. Fences and hedges give a garden an instant setting. Their enclosure provides a personal space, with privacy and shelter, where the plants that you choose can be seen against the backdrop that suits them best. Within a garden, subdivisions of the plot can create different areas, where each will have its own atmosphere, so barriers are also invaluable as mood changers.

Because nothing else is so important to the structure of a garden, what you use for the divisions both around and within your plot deserves careful consideration. Hedges need more space than fences, but they would always be my first choice. A good two-metres (6 ft) tall hedge, that stops people looking in or seeing out, will take up a little

less than two metres (6 ft) of growing ground, because although the hedge itself only needs half of this amount, the gap on either side will be virtually dead ground. It is difficult to grow flowers where they have to compete with the hungry roots of an established hedge and the space will anyway be useful for maintenance of the hedge, which will need at least an annual cut. If there is room for a planted barrier, consider yew rather than the Leyland cypress, which is not a good choice for an evergreen hedge. Leyland cypress grows fast and needs constant cutting if it is to be manageable, and will ultimately occupy far more ground than yew. If it is encouraged and watered in its infancy, yew grows 25 cm (1 ft) a year, and it needs but one trim annually. It makes the perfect backdrop for any plant.

Where a permanent barrier is chosen, find one that suits your style. Smart trellis for formal gardens and town plots; wattle for the rustic at heart; walls for those who live in stony places; wood for traditionalists; there is something to suit every gardener. Even chain link fencing can be acceptable with an overcoat of ivy, and indeed all of these 'built' barriers will support a host of climbers.

ABOVE Sometimes in a garden a temporary screen has to be arranged – to keep people off the grass perhaps, or animals from charging through seedlings. Here an effective barrier has been made out of bent hazel wands and bamboo canes to protect a fragile area near the path. It could be used too as a climbing frame for peas. Another stop-gap in this style is a miniature sheep hurdle, the sort of thing that can be used to remind people not to take a short cut across a worn patch of grass. These are gentle reminders, not 'Halt-who-goes-there' statements.

RIGHT Netting, like a veil on an old-fashioned hat, hangs over strawberries making them look even more alluring than they do without it. Fruit, unless it is strictly for the birds, has to be netted, but, like all the stages in a working garden's life, the precaution also has its charms.

ABOVE The step-over apple tree, seen in the background of the vegetables here, is a miniature, single-tier version of the espalier trees found in larger gardens. It makes a neat edge to the workmanlike rows of crops, separating them from the lawn and flower beds beyond. Most plants respond to having their branches tied down, so that they form a right angle to the stem by producing more fruit (or flowers) than they would if allowed to grow in a more vertical position. This encourages them to produce masses of fruit-carrying side shoots, along the upper side of the horizontal stem.

NEAR RIGHT In places where very little will grow because of space or light, or problems with the soil, the plainest of plantings can be given dash with a colourful fence. Here, ironwork pots of cornflowers guard a town garden. If they had nothing else growing behind them under the shady tree, they would still make a cheerful garden picture.

NEAR RIGHT, CENTRE Painting on a wooden house is echoed in the green and white-tipped fence. Paint can be the gardener's ally, giving a sophisticated look for a town garden fence, or a traditional one for the country.

NEAR RIGHT, BELOW This treatment might be too elegant for a cottage garden. Dahlias, salvias and African marigolds cluster around a simple fence stained orange.

FAR RIGHT A cat adds the finishing touch to this fence, where greens and whites are seen with a touch of snow. The modern-looking posts suggest a garden where one might find architectural plants – such as bamboos or grasses. Like entrances, fences should give a hint of what lies within their bounds.

ABOVE Built walls can often seem hard-edged in a garden if they are not clothed in plants. But sometimes a wall is too beautiful to cover, like this combination of flint topped with bricks, where snapdragons have settled. As an alternative to climbers, which cover large surfaces of wall, plants that colonize a wall and live comfortably in its crevices allow the stonework to be seen. They suggest, far more convincingly than a trained rose would do, that the wall is part of the living landscape. Sadly, this picture has to come with a health-and-safety warning. Although wall-flowers, valerian, snapdragons and the like are delightful growing in this way, they will not prolong the life of the wall. Ivy, the plant that really makes itself at home among brick and stones, should be discour-aged. Ultimately its roots (which are stronger than those of the plants above), will damage the mortar joints and pull any wall apart.

ABOVE Rock plants are perfectly suited to life among the stones in a dry stone wall, where no cement has been used in the joints. Conditions here are a passable imitation of the plants' natural alpine home. Drainage is good, because the water runs quickly off and through the stones, but roots that like a cool place can find pockets of earth out of the sun. Although the small stone trough looks as though it offers similar conditions to the wall below it, this is misleading. Shallow stone troughs allow no escape from the sun, so these are not the best places for plants that like to keep their roots cool. Stone crops, however, as their name suggests, will thrive here without any attention. House leeks would do equally well, as they too can survive drought. It is possible in such dry conditions to grow plants that need more cossetting than these succulents, but they would have to be watered daily.

TOP Simple wooden fences make a tidy and practical edging for vegetables that need protection from animals. It is important to sink some netting underground if rabbits are to be completely deterred, as they are not daunted by digging under a fence to get at the lettuces.

ABOVE Iron railings like these were common in Victorian gardens, particularly in towns. They add a note of old-fashioned strength, but they do need regular painting if they are not to go rusty, so their maintenance is more demanding than that of most fences.

RIGHT The post and rails at the back of this flower bed would be good in a larger country garden, but the arrangement could look rather heavy and overwhelming for a small-scale plot. Rustic fencing such as this was popular with nineteenth-century gardeners.

LEFT Behind the table and chair, a neat trellis made of light slats of wood suits a town garden. The narrow rectangular spaces between the bars make a change from the more usual diamond- or square-shaped trellis, the standard patterns for shop-bought trellis.

Entrances

Entrances are one of the few points in the garden where you can control the view. Most of the time, a garden is seen on the move. There is no certainty that the place where one person stops to admire the plants will grab the attention of another. So the only checks on a circuit of the flowers are seats and entrances. Seats can be ignored by the garden visitor, but entrances have to be used. The pause on the threshold to look at what lies beyond can be the most thrilling experience in the garden. Everyone knows that secret gardens are at their best when seen from the entrance, but that once inside, the spell soon evaporates. The gate to a garden should allow a view into the world beyond, so that as the barrier is opened the gaze is held and that moment of anticipation is prolonged. The arch over a half-height gate is the best arrangement of all because it frames the view and makes it even more special (above and far right). Another trick to heighten the drama is to ensure that the gate opens away from you, leading the onlooker into the picture. With all this stage management it would be a waste to make the area beyond the gate the same in feeling as the one about to be left.

The width and height of the entrance is important; too high and narrow and it will seem forbidding; too broad and low and it will appear insignificant. Choose materials that are in evidence in the rest of the garden or in sympathy with the style. Brick piers, for example, are for gardens where brick is the dominant building material. Wooden gates will certainly do for rustic settings, but well-finished and painted they can seem right anywhere.

Woven hurdles, like these, were used in early gardens to keep winds and beasts away from crops and flowers. Medieval illustrations show stout posts with willow shoots wound around them in much the same way as the ones in the picture; but for those who do not want to go through the whole medieval process, wattle hurdles do not need to be made at home to look convincingly traditional. Like all artefacts made from natural materials, they never look out of place out of doors, but wattle is perhaps a better material to choose for a country garden than for one in the heart of a town.

Larch-lap is another form of woven fencing that is more often seen and used than wattle. When tall panels of either of these materials are used, they must be well secured to posts driven at least 45 cm (18 in) into the ground. The wind can play havoc with solid panels above about 1.5 m (5 ft) in height, so firm anchorage is essential. Larch-lap is more closely woven than wattle, so the nasturtiums that are creeping through the fence here would not be able to decorate an expanse of larch-lap as they do the wattle.

But larch-lap and similar wooden overlapping fences do make better hosts for climbing plants than wattle. Nails and wires are hard to fix on the rippled surface of wattle, which allows plants too many crevices to creep into. On solid panels they can be pinned and displayed to best advantage. Roses, for example, need a strong backing that would be hard to provide on a wattle hurdle, but modern woven fencing gives them the support they need.

Directory of Illustrated Plants

It would be impossible to list every plant illustrated in every picture, since many plants merge into the background or are indistinct. The following lists those plants that feature prominently in the photographs; plant names marked* are not necessarily positive identifications, but would achieve the effect of the plant illustrated.

Page 6
Narcissus 'Tête-à-Tête'

Page 7
Front right (in trough): *Cotoneaster**

Page 8
Front left (fine leaves): *Foeniculum vulgare*, fennel
Centre (hedge): *Berberis thunbergii* f. *atropurpurea*

Page 9, left
Clematis 'Niobe'

Page 9, right
Front: *Pelargonium* 'Hederinum'*

Pages 10-11
Front (behind basin): *Plantago media*, hoary plantain
Centre, left: *Taxus baccata*, common yew
Centre, rear (tree): *Pinus mugo*

Page 11, top
Cactus dahlia

Page 11, bottom
Salix alba, white willow (pollarded)

Page 14
Right (low-spreading tree) *Hamamelis* 'Pallida'*

Pages 14-15
Foreground: *Magnolia* x *soulangeana*

Page 16, top
Front left: *Fragaria* x *ananassa*, strawberry
Centre (against log): *Tropaeolum majus*, nasturtium

Page 16, bottom
Far left (tall, upright plant): *Kniphofia* 'Atlanta'*
Rear centre (tree): *Acer negundo* 'Variegatum'
Centre (main ground cover): *Acaena* 'Blue Haze'*
Front centre (orange flower): *Meconopsis cambrica* var. *aurantiaca*

Page 17, top
Left (yellow flower): *Cephalaria gigantea*
Centre (yellow flower): *Oenothera biennis*
Right (yellow flower): *Inula helenium*

Page 18
Rear right: *Rosa* 'Buff Beauty'*

Page 19, top
Rear (against wall): *Acanthus spinosus*
Front right (yellow-flowering herb): *Foeniculum vulgare*, fennel

Page 19, bottom left
Front left: *Felicia amoena**
Front of table: *Exacum affine*
Rear of table: *Brachyscome iberidifolia*

Pages 20-1
Front (red flower): *Astilbe* 'Fanal'*
Left (tall white flower): *Verbascum nigrum*
Centre left and right (purple flower): *Phlox paniculata* 'Elizabeth Campbell'
Rear left (grass): *Deschampsia flexuosa*
Centre right (pink flower): *Hemerocallis* 'Pink Damask', daylily
Centre right (red flower): *Hemerocallis* 'Stafford'

Page 22, left
Front left: *Raphiolepsis* x *delacourii**

Page 22, right
Left (climber, large leaves): *Parthenocissus quinquefolia*, Virginia creeper
Right (in pot): *Hosta sieboldiana* 'Frances Williams'

Page 23, top
Box sofa: *Buxus sempervirens*
Right (hedge): *Acer campestre**

Pages 24-5, top
Front left (large green leaves): rhubarb
Front left (pink flower): *Paeonia lactiflora*
Rear left (tall, purple flower): *Delphinium* sp.
Top right (tree climbing over path): pear
Centre right (red flower): *Paeonia lactiflora*
Front right (purple flower): *Nepeta* 'Six Hills Giant'

Pages 24-5, bottom
(pink flower): *Polygonum bistorta* 'Superba'

Pages 28-9
Right (long grass): *Deschampsia cespitosa**

Page 29
Growing on statue: *Jovibarba* x *hirta**

Page 30, left
Aconitum hemsleyanum

Page 33, right
Taxus baccata, common yew

Page 34
Front left (pink flower): *Rosa* 'Blessings'
Centre (small, yellow flower): *Sanicula europaea*
Right: *Papaver somniferum*, peony-flowered poppy

Page 35
Around tree: *Lobelia*
Tree: *Picea pungens*

Page 36, left
Cobaea scandens

Pages 36-7
(white flower): *Lychnis chalcedonica* 'Alba'

Page 37
(yellow flower): *Nymphoïdes peltata*
(water lily): *Nymphaea* sp.

Page 39, bottom
Left (in pots): citrus
(yellow flower): *Phlomis fruticosa*

Page 40
Wall climber: *Hedera colchica* 'Dentata Variegata'

Page 43, left
Begonias

Page 43, top right
Solenostemon scutellarioïdes, coleus

Page 43, bottom right
Left: Zinnia
Right: *Tagetes tenuifolia*

Pages 44-5
Left and right: *Digitalis purpurea*, Foxy Hybrids

Page 46, top
Argyranthemum 'Petite Pink'

Page 46, bottom
Main ground cover: *Ajuga pyramidalis*
Rear (pink flower): *Dicentra* sp.*
Centre (in dish): *Viola tricolor*

Page 47, bottom right
Tree: *Brugmansia* x *candida* 'Knightii'

Page 48, bottom
Plant surrounding tree: *Symphytum grandiflorum*

Pages 48-9
(bottom step, left): *Sedum* sp.
(second step, left): *Sedum acre*
(second step, right): *Sedum* sp.
(third step): *Jovibarba* x *hirta*
(fourth step): *Sedum spathulifolium*
(top step): *Thymus* sp.
Right (covering steps): *Hedera helix*

Page 49, right
Macleaya x *kewensis**

Pages 50-1, top
Lavandula angustifolia

Pages 50-1, bottom left
Impatiens

Pages 50-1, bottom right:
Front centre: *Hedera helix*
Front right: *Lythrum virgatum*
Rear right: *Miscanthus* sp.

Page 52, top
Left (rust-coloured leaves): *Acer palmatum*
Centre (behind pots): *Mahonia* x *wagneri*

Pages 52-3, bottom
Left of stone trough: *Hosta sieboldiana*
Rear centre: *Hedera colchica* *
Flowers in trough: *Viola tricolor* 'Prince Henry'
Far right: *Hydrangea*

Page 53, top right
Centre (in pot): *Heuchera micrantha* 'Palace Purple'
Right: *Papaver somniferum*, opium poppy

Page 53, bottom left
Left: *Lavandula angustifolia*
Right: *Salvia officinalis* Purpurascens Group

Page 53, bottom right
Lilium regale Album Group

Page 54
Topiary bird: *Buxus sempervirens*

Pages 56-7, top
Trees: *Tilia cordata**
Hedge: *Buxus sempervirens* 'Suffruticosa'

Page 58, bottom
Ivy: *Hedera helix* 'Oro di Bogliasco' ('Goldheart')

Page 59, top
Growing round bench: *Buxus sempervirens*

Page 59, bottom left
Ligustrum ovalifolium 'Aureum' (golden privet)

Page 59, bottom right
Trees: *Laurus nobilis*

Page 60, top left
Rear (three bushes): *Santolina pinnata*
Centre and right (purple flower): *Nigella damascena*, love-in-a-mist
Front (yellow flower): *Argyranthemum* 'Jamaica Primrose'

Page 60, bottom
Front centre: *Salix hastata* 'Wehrhahnii'*
Left: *Salix elaeagnos*
Rear: *Buxus sempervirens*

Pages 60-1
Rear (tree): *Pinus* sp.

Page 61
Front (in pots): *Buxus sempervirens*
Rear (in front of hedge): *Euphorbia characias*

Page 62, top left
Standards: *Viburnum carlesii*

Page 62, bottom left
Hedge: *Buxus sempervirens*, common box

Pages 62-3, top
Trees: *Ilex aquifolium* 'J.C. van Tol'
Hedge: *Taxus baccata*, common yew

Pages 62-3, bottom
Front: *Hosta*
Centre: *Hedera helix*, arborescent form of common ivy
Rear: *Parthenocissus tricuspidata*

Page 66, top
Hedge: *Ligustrum ovalifolium*, hedging privet

Page 66, bottom
Topiary stag: *Ligustrum ovalifolium* 'Aureum'

Page 67, top
Rear (hedge): *Fagus sylvaticum*, common beech
Far right (topiary shape): *Taxus baccata*, common yew

Page 68
Left: *Dryopteris filix-mas*, male fern
Centre: *Verbascum olympicum*
Right (orange flower): *Ligularia* x *palmatiloba*
Right (white flower): *Verbascum nigrum*

Page 69
Centranthus ruber, red valerian

156

Page 70
At four corners of low hedge: *Santolina chamaecyparissus*
Centre: *Cynara cardunculus* Scolymus Group, globe artichoke

Pages 70-1
Inside hedges: *Crambe cordifolia*

Page 71
Agave americana

Page 72
Lavatera trimestris 'Silver Cup'

Pages 72-3
Rear (pink flower): *Rhododendron* sp
Front: *Meconopsis* x *sheldonii*

Page 73, top
Around tree: *Crocus vernus*

Page 73, bottom
Front: *Tulipa* 'Flaming Parrot'

Pages 74-5
Centre left to right (tallest plant): *Verbascum olympicum*
Centre left (tall stems, round heads): *Papaver somniferum*, opium poppy
Centre (herb): *Foeniculum vulgare*, fennel
Left and right (white flower): *Rosa* 'Iceberg'

Page 76, top
Fern: *Matteuccia struthiopteris*

Page 76, bottom
Alcea rosea, hollyhock

Pages 76-7
Heracleum mantegazzianum, giant hogweed

Page 78, left
Front: *Rosa rugosa*

Page 78, right
Allium christophii with *Asperula*, *Nigella* and *Viola*

Pages 78-9, top
Front left: *Sedum* 'Herbstfreude' ('Autumn Joy')*
Rear left and front right: *Yucca*

Pages 78-9
(seed heads): *Scabiosa stellata*

Page 80, top
Rear left: *Rheum palmatum*
Front centre: *Lobelia* x *speciosa*
Rear right: *Rubus* sp.

Page 80, bottom
Eucomis bicolor

Page 81, top
Centre (red stalk): Ruby chard

Page 81, bottom
Left to right (white flower): *Acanthus mollis*

Page 85, top left
Tree arching over path: pear
Left (white flower): *Iris* 'Florentina'

Page 85, bottom
(tall spikes): leek

Page 86, left
(plant under window): *Impatiens glandulifera*, Himalayan balsam

Page 86, right
(in pans): *Sempervivum* cvs

Page 87, top
Front centre (pink flower): *Verbena tenuisecta*
Left (yellow-flowering herb): *Foeniculum vulgare*, fennel
Centre right: heliotrope

Page 87, bottom right
(behind basket): *Lavandula angustifolia* 'Hidcote Pink'*

Page 88
Left: Brussels sprouts
Right: red oak-leaf lettuce

Pages 88-9, top
Left and centre (yellow flower): *Verbascum nigrum*

Page 94,
Primula vulgaris, primrose

Pages 94-5
Front: *Gymnocarpium dryopteris*, oak fern
Rear: *Acer palmatum* f. *atropurpureum*

Page 95, bottom right
Centre left: iris
Centre (tree): *Pinus* sp.
Rear right (white flower): *Anemone* x *hybrida* 'Honorine Jobert'*

Pages 98-9, left
Centre, left to right: *Dianthus barbatus*, sweet William
Rear right (yellow flower): *Rosa* 'Laurence Johnston'*

Pages 98-9,
Left of centre: 'Zéphirine Drouhin'

Pages 98-9, bottom
Wisteria sinensis

Page 100, top
Wall climber: *Vitis vinifera*

Pages 100-1
Front: Zinnias
Centre (pink flower): *Lavatera trimestris*

Page 102, top
Growing round frame: sweet pea

Page 106, left
At base of left plant support: *Hosta* sp.
Growing round plant support: lime

Page 110
Hydrangea macrophylla

Pages 110-11, top
Centre (left and right of path): Lavender
Roses: *Rosa* 'Iceberg'
Rear (around) urn: potato

Pages 110-11, bottom left
Left and right of path: *Soleirolia soleirolii*, mind-your-own-business or curse of Corsica

Pages 112-13, left
First plant to right of path: *Alchemilla mollis*

Page 113, top
Tree (white blossom): cherry*

Page 113, bottom
Rear left: *Rosa* 'Frühlingsgold'*

Page 114, bottom
Front left (small, pink flower): *Lamium maculatum*
Centre (yellow flower): *Doronicum orientale* 'Goldzwerg'*

Page 115
Front left (yellow flower): *Verbascum* sp.
Left (pink flower): *Scabiosa columbaria*
Rear centre (pink flower): *Salvia sclarea* var. *turkestanica*
Rear right (yellow flower): *Inula helenium*
Rear right (purple flower): *Nepeta sibirica*
Main plant to right of path: *Gypsophila*
Front (arching across path): *Coronilla varia*
Front right (yellow flower): *Coreopsis verticillata*

Page 118
Front left: *Papaver orientale*, oriental poppy

Pages 118-19
Main ground cover: *Anthemis punctata* subsp. *cupaniana*
Rear right: *Tussilago farfara*, coltsfoot*

Page 119, top right
Flowers: *Erigeron kavinskianus*
Right (fern): *Asplenium scolopendrium* (*Phyllitis scolopendrium*)

Page 119, bottom
Covering steps: *Fragaria vesca*

Page 120
(foreground:) *Rosa* 'Albertine'
Centre right: *Lavatera* 'Rosea'
Rear right: *Ficus carica*, fig

Page 121
Right (against window): *Rubus fruticosus* 'Oregon Thornless'*
(red flower): *Clematis* 'Niobe'*

Page 122, right
Right of path (tall, yellow flower): *Verbascum olympicum*

Page 123
Top left: *Rosa* 'New Dawn'
Centre (pink flower): *Petunia*

Page 124, left
Left: *Rosa multiflora*
Right (on ledge): *Echeveria secunda* var. *glauca*

Pages 124-5
Left (yellow flower): *Thalictrum flavum* ssp. *glaucum*
Rear centre (purple flower): *Delphinium*
Centre right (red flower): *Lychnis chalcedonica*

Pages 126-7
Front (white flower): *Verbascum nigrum*

Page 127, top
(pink flower): *Acanthus spinosus*

Page 127, bottom
Left: *Rosa* 'Golden Wings'

Page 128
(orange flower): *Lilium* x *dalhansonii*
Front centre (low ground cover): *Tiarella cordifolia*
Right (end of bed): *Sarcococca* sp.

Page 129, bottom left
Tree: *Quercus rubra**

Page 129, bottom right
Left (tall, yellow flower): *Anthemis tinctoria*
Right (yellow flower): *Alchemilla mollis*

Page 130, top
Vine: *Vitis vinifera*
Front left: *Hesperis matronalis*, sweet rocket

Page 130, bottom
Centre (yellow/green leaves): *Humulus lupulus* 'Aureus'*
Right (ground cover): *Teucrium scorodonia**

Pages 130-1, top
(pink flower): *Epilobium angustifolium*
(yellow flower): *Buphthalmum speciosum*

Page 132
Front right: *Papaver somniferum*, opium poppy

Pages 134-5, bottom
Centre left of pond: *Gymnocarpium robertianum**
Front right (white flower): *Sedum album**

Page 135, bottom
Front left: *Acanthus*
Rear centre (large leaves): *Macleaya* sp.

Page 136, left
Front centre: *Milium effusum* 'Aureum', Bowles's golden grass

Page 138, top
Left: *Anthriscus cerefolium*, cow parsley*
Right (fern): *Matteuccia struthiopteris*

Page 138, bottom
Front left: *Iris* 'Snowdrift'*

Page 138- 9, top
Rear (orange flower): *Primula bulleyana*
Rear right (tall, red flower): *Primula florindae* and *P. waltonii*

Page 140
Against fence (orange flower): *Fritillaria imperialis* 'Rubra Maxima', crown imperial

Page 141
Eschscholzia californica, Californian poppy

Page 142
Centre (tall, round heads): leek
Front (ground cover): *Salvia officinalis* Purpurascens Group

Page 143, top
Centre: red cabbage
Behind cabbage: leek
Centre right (purple leaves): *Salvia officinalis* Purpurascens Group

Page 144, bottom
In front of fence (red flower): *Zinnia*

Page 146
Antirrhinum majus, snapdragon

Page 147
Centre (white flowers): *Saxifraga* sp.*
Right (yellow flower): *Corydalis lutea*

Page 148, bottom
Left: *Oxalis articulata*
Centre: *Tanacetum parthenium*, feverfew

Page 149, top
Top centre: *Vitis vinifera* 'Purpurea'
Centre right (pink flower): *Clematis* 'Kermesina'*

Page 150, top
Left (ground cover): *Alchemilla mollis*

Page 150, bottom
Centre (yellow flower): *Helleborus foetidus* Wester Flisk Group

Page 151, top right
Rear: *Rosa* 'Albertine'
(hedge): *Ligustrum ovalifolium* 'Aureum'

Page 151, bottom right
Arching over gate: *Carpinus betulus*, hornbeam

Pages 152-3
Growing over fence: *Tropaeolum majus*, nasturtium

Index

Acknowledgments

Marijke Heuff and the publisher would like to thank the following garden owners and designers for allowing us to reproduce photographs of their gardens:

1 Balbithan House, Scotland; 2-3 Great Dixter, Sussex; 3 right Cilia Prenen; 5-6 Marijke Heuff; 7 Palaccio de Viana, Spain; 9 left Mrs C. Bader-Heemskerk; 10-11 Mrs M. van Bennekom-Scheffer; 11 above right Gardens Mien Ruys; 12 Giardini: Walda Pairon; 13 Mrs C. G. Lancaster, The Coach House, Little Haseley, Oxfordshire; 14 left Mrs H. J. van Puijenbroek; 14-15 Mrs L.Goossenaerts-Miedma; 16 above The Priona Gardens; 16 centre Mr and Mrs Eschauzier van Rood; 16 below Designer: Els de Boer; 17 above Bellingeweer; 17 below Mr and Mrs Brinkworth-Makeham; 18 Mr and Mrs Molesworth, Balmoral, Benenden, Kent; 19 above Marjolein Weyers; 19 below left Ineke Greve; 19 below right Marijke Heuff; 20-21 Ton ter Linden; 22 left Giardini: Walda Pairon; 22 right Designer: Marcel Wolterinck; 23 above Mrs M. van Bennekom-Scheffer; 23 below Mrs Cartwright-Hignett, Iford Manor, Bradford-on-Avon, Wiltshire (near Bath); 24 left Ineke Greve; 24-5 above Garden designed by Mary Keen, Berkshire; 24-5 below Mrs M. van Bennekom-Scheffer; 26 Jaap Nieuwenhuis and Paula Thies (Trompe l'oeil designed by Jaap Nieuwenhuis); 27 Giardini: Walda Pairon; 28-9 Jaap Nieuwenhuis and Paula Thies (Trompe l'oeil designed by Jaap Nieuwenhuis); 29 right Designers: Lia and Jorn Copijn; 30 Designer: Bep Aten; 31 Frans Smeets; 32 above left Mrs L. Goossenaerts-Miedma (Sculpture by Evert de Hartog); 32-3 above Giardini: Walda Pairon; 33 above right Mr and Mrs Brinkworth-Makeham; 33 right Mr and Mrs James Sellick, Pashley Manor, Ticehurst, Sussex; 34 Mr and Mrs Bijen-Menwessen; 36 left Mrs L.Goossenaerts-Miedma (Sculpture by Evert de Hartog); 36-7 Ineke Greve; 37 right Mr and Mrs Helsen-Buurman; 38-9 above Mr and Mrs Eschauzier-van Rood; 38-9 below The Priona Gardens; 39 above right Bellingeweer; 39 below right Mr and Mrs Hugh Johnson, Saling Hall, Great Saling, Essex; 40 Designer: Anthony Noel, London; 42 Trix Boterman; 43 below right Huis Bingerden; 44-45 Designer: Marcel Wolterinck; 46 above Sissinghurst Place Gardens, Sussex; 46 below Mr and Mrs van der Upwich-Koffler; 47 below left Garden Mien Ruys; 47 below right Mrs C. G. Lancaster, The Coach House, Little Haseley, Oxfordshire; 48 above left Mr and Mrs R. R. Merton, The Old Rectory, Burghfield, Berkshire; 48 below Hetty Cox; 49 right Marijke Jansen; 50 left Mrs C. G. Lancaster, The Coach House, Little Haseley, Oxfordshire; 50-1 above Designer: Marcel Wolterinck; 52-3 above Mrs L. Goossenaerts-Miedma; 52 below Hof van Walenburg; 53 above right Sijtje Stuurman; 53 below right The Priona Gardens; 54 Hetty Cox; 56-7 Mr J. van den Brink; 57 right, 58 and 59 above Ineke Greve; 59 below right Mr and Mrs Braam-Holierwoek; 60 above left Peter and Pam Lewis, Stickey Wicket, Buckland Newton, Dorset; 60 below left Mr and Mrs Hugh Johnson, Saling Hall, Great Saling, Essex; 60-1 Mr and Mrs Compeer van der Werf; 61 right Mrs M. van Bennekom-Scheffer; 62 above left Patricia van Roosmalen; 62 below Mrs C.G. Lancaster, The Coach House, Little Haseley, Oxfordshire; 62-3 above Koelemeyers Gardens; 62-3 below Mrs M. van Bennekom-Scheffer; 64 above Mr and Mrs Adriaanse-Quint; 64 below Mr and Mrs Groenewegen-Groot; 65 above Mrs L.Goossenaerts-Miedma; 65 below Huis Bingerden; 66-7 above Mr and Mrs van Heuven-Waldkotter; 66 below Giardini: Walda Pairon; 67 below Designer/Sculptor: Miep Maarse; 68 Mrs M. van Bennekom-Scheffer; 69 Garden designed by Mary Keen, Berkshire; 70 above Mrs M. van Bennekom-Scheffer; 71 above Mr and Mrs Eshauzier van Rood; 70-1 below Mr and Mrs Braam-Holierhoek; 73 above right Mr and Mrs Hansems-Poorthuis; 73 below right Loekie Schwartz; 74-5 The Priona Gardens; 76 above left Sijtje Stuurman; 76 below left Riet Brinkhof; 76-7 Mr and Mrs Bynen-Henrard; 78-9 above Mrs C.G.Lancaster, The Coach House, Little Haseley, Oxfordshire; 78 below left Mrs M. van Beenkom-Scheffer; 78 below centre The Priona Gardens; 78-9 below K.Salim Seeds; 80 above N. & S. Pope, Hadspen Gardens, Castle Cary, Somerset; 80 below Maria de Haan; 81 above Gardens Mien Ruys; 81 below Casa de Pilatos, Spain; 83 Ineke Greve; 84 and 85 above left Garden designed by Mary Keen, Berkshire; 85 above right and below N. & S. Pope, Hadspen Gardens, Castle Cary, Somerset; 86 left Riet Brinkhof; 86 right Mr F.Greew and Mr F.Tiebout; 86 below Sitjte Stuurman; 87 above N. & S. Pope, Hadspen Gardens, Castle Cary, Somerset; 88 left Cilia Prenen; 88-9 The Priona Gardens; 89 below right Designer: Marc de Winter; 90 above N. & S. Pope, Hadspen Gardens, Castle Cary, Somerset; 90 below Mr and Mrs Eschauzier van Rood; 91 Hetty Cox; 92 above left Paula Thies and Jaap Nieuwenhuis; 92-3 below Els Raats; 94 Mr and Mrs van der Upwich-Koffler; 94-5 Kildrummy, Scotland; 95 above right Bellingeweer; 95 below right Mr and Mrs Arnold-Overbeeke; 96 Patricia van Roosmalen; 97 Mrs C.G.Lancaster, The Coach House, Little Haseley, Oxfordshire; 98-9 Mr and Mrs J.Jempson, Cleveland House, Winchelsea, Sussex; 99 below Loeki Schwartz; 100 above left Mr and Mrs Hugh Johnson, Saling Hall, Great Saling, Essex; 100 below left Hetty Cox; 100-1 Huis Bingerden; 102 above Mr and Mrs Bicker Caarten-Wiersum (Designer: Els Proost); 102 below Gardens Mien Ruys; 103 Ton ter Linden; 104-5 Mr and Mrs Degeyter (Designer: P. Deroose); 106 left Patricia van Roosmalen; 106 centre Castle Wylre; 106-7 Mr and Mrs P.R.Styles, Brookwell, Bramley, Surrey; 109 Hetty Cox; 110-111 above Ineke Greve; 110-111 below Designer: Anthony Noel, London; 111 below right Mrs R. Sieber: 112-3 Mrs C.G. Lancaster, The Coach House, Little Haseley, Oxfordshire; 113 above Great Dixter, Sussex; 113 below Mr and Mrs Simon Gault, Field Farm, Iden Green, Kent; 114 above left Mr M. van der Upwich; 114 above right N. & S. Pope, Hadspen Gardens, Castle Cary, Somerset; 114 below Mirjam Hart-Nyburg; 115 The Priona Gardens; 117 above right Frans Smeets; 118 above left Mrs L. Goossenaerts-Miedema; 118 below left Great Wad, Frittenden, Kent; 118-9 Borde Hill Garden, Sussex; 119 above right Kerdalo, France; 119 below right and 120 Garden designed by Mary Keen, Berkshire; 121 Sijtje Stuurman; 122 left Borde Hill Garden, Sussex; 122 right Garden designed by Mary Keen, Berkshire; 123 Sijtje Stuurman; 124 left Riet Brinkhof; 124-5 Maria Hofker-Rueter; 126 left Mr and Mrs Eschauzier van Rood; 127 above right Mr and Mrs Menken-Kreiter; 127 below right Mr and Mrs Brinkworth-Makeham; 128 Tintinhull, Somerset; 129 above Mr and Mrs Eschauzier-van Rood; 129 below left Mr and Mrs Degeyter; 130 above left Mrs C.G.Lancaster, The Coach House, Little Haseley, Oxfordshire; 130 below left Threave Gardens, Scotland; 130-1 above Mr and Mrs Degeyter (Designer: P.Deroose); 132 Bellingeweer; 133 Mr and Mrs Arnold-Overbeeke; 134-5 above Gardens Miens Ruys; 134-5 below Mr and Mrs Janette Walen-Wilson; 135 above right Mr and Mrs Eshauzier van Rood; 135 below Mr F.de Greew and Mr F.Tibout; 136 left Designer: Anthony Noel, London; 136 right Castle Groot-Buggenum; 137 Dirk Jan Koning; 138 above left Mr J. de Jager; 138 below Mr and Mrs Arnold-Overbeeke; 138-9 above Mr and Mrs Noel Gibbs, Combend Manor, Elkstone, Gloucestershire; 139 below Mr and Mrs Molesworth, Balmoral, Benenden, Kent; 142-3 above N. & S. Pope, Hadspen Gardens, Castle Cary, Somerset; 143 below Broncynhinta, Pont Robert; 147 Balbithan House, Scotland; 149 above Marijke Heuff; 149 below Irene Jansen; 150 above Ineke Greve; 150 below Mrs L.Goossenaerts-Miedma; 151 above left Mr and Mrs Melick-van Walsum; 151 below left Ineke Greve; 151 below right Mr and Mrs Molesworth, Balmoral, Benenden, Kent; 152-3 Nursery de Kleine Plantage.

Index by Yvonne McCara